LEARN BEGINNER'S ITALIAN GRAMMAR WORKBOOK

TABLE OF CONTENTS

DISCLAIMER NOTICE:

Please note the information contained within this document is for educational and entertainment purposes only. All effort has been executed to present accurate, up to date, reliable, complete information. No warranties of any kind are declared or implied. Readers acknowledge that the author is not engaged in the rendering of legal, financial, medical or professional advice. The content within this book has been derived from various sources. Please consult a licensed professional before

attempting any techniques outlined in this book. By reading this document, the reader agrees that under no circumstances is the author responsible for any losses, direct or indirect, that are incurred as a result of the use of the information contained within this document, including, but not limited to, errors, omissions, or inaccuracies.

Speak Abroad
Academy

INTRODUCTION

Let me guess that you're interested in learning Italian, and you've tried formal lessons and apps, but you're stuck. You don't know why. No matter how excited you are at the beginning, you always end up losing your motivation. You start having difficulty finding time to sit and practice until you finally give up. Will you ever be able to learn Italian?

Of course, you will! While we all know that learning a new language requires effort and commitment, you will regain your motivation and look forward to learning with the right approach.

So, what is the right approach?

Scheduling a time for lessons is a great way to keep your motivation high. But this will only happen if learning is pleasant and easy; that is, if you're not overwhelmed by new information. You will be excited about new content and tasks if you feel you're in control of the process.

That is precisely what we have undertaken with this workbook: delivering micro lessons with tiny pieces of information. By providing simple-to-follow lessons and lots—yes, lots! —of practice, the Beginner Italian Grammar Workbook will help you learn Italian quickly and thoroughly. Our online easy-to-follow workbook engages readers from the very first page with short, to-the-point grammar explanations and fun exercises. Our program has put you, the learner, at the center of the learning journey, keeping in mind that every day you have a long list of tasks competing for your time and energy. Italian should not be placed on the overflowing to-do list that fills people with stress and anxiety. Instead, it should be an enjoyable activity you turn to when you want to relax and distract yourself. Think of learning a language in the same way as doing exercise: if you want it to stick, you need to make it pleasurable. When you're enjoying the learning process, it feels effortless—even though, many times, it isn't! — and you learn the new language more effectively.

The Beginner Italian Grammar Workbook helps you build Italian into your life by learning words in context, as they appear naturally, and presenting grammar explanations in real-life situations. You'll pick up your vocabulary from short stories and everyday scenes and songs. The extensive practice applies the concepts learned and reviews what you have already mastered. Our bite-sized lessons are based on gradual, cumulative learning: each new class builds on the previous ones to keep you from forgetting earlier notions. It's called "baby steps." You will constantly review what you know as you take in new knowledge. This has the two-fold benefit of boosting self-confidence as you train your brain to recognize new language patterns. When you start identifying and remembering past lessons, you will feel that you're finally making progress.

Our *Beginner Italian Grammar Workbook* has helped hundreds of people who have started reading and writing Italian only weeks after beginning the program. Many have travelled to Italian country, enhancing their travel experience. Others have increased their job prospects and tell us that learning Italian has opened doors to job opportunities they would have never applied for before, even if they just have basic proficiency in Italian. And others are excited about gaining a greater appreciation for Italian culture. When you read and understand Italian, you start enjoying Italian art, theatre, music, film, literature, podcasts, and blogs in their original forms and with an insider's perspective.

As you begin your lessons with our Beginner Italian Grammar Workbook, you will feel a sense of accomplishment because of how each class is structured. Clear explanations of grammatical rules and exercises that connect directly will help you make quick strides to push you forward. As you practice what you learn, you will gain confidence and feel motivated to move on to the next step. Before you know it, you will start to express your thoughts and feelings in Italian and understand the variety of Italian-language resources. We provide excerpts from poems, songs, and social media, among others. You will read and write in Italian, using your newly acquired skills wherever you go.

Our Beginner **Italian** Grammar Workbook aims to keep you focused and on track. Instead of asking you to carve out a considerable amount of time for studying, you'll be engaging in short, easy lessons. You won't feel overwhelmed because the lessons are brief and focused. Each class highlights one grammar issue at a time and makes sure you practice it. Our exercises include a wide variety of topics and respond to current trends. In addition, each new grammar concept builds on the previous ones, making sure you review what you know before jumping into new content.

So why wait any longer? Start right now! Boost your Italian learning today with our Beginner Italian Grammar Workbook and step into a lifetime of possibilities: new friends, exciting trips, and a host of career-growth opportunities.

LESSON 01

GOOD MORNING AND GOODBYE

SUBJECT PRONOUNS

First things first! The first step to learning any language always begins with subject pronouns. In English, these are words like 'I,' 'You,' and 'They.' They indicate *who* exactly we're talking about and they're essential for everyday conversation! Without them, it would be impossible to describe ourselves, other people, and how events have affected us. They are some of the most basic building blocks of any language.

So, let's take a look at what subject pronouns in **Italian** are!

1 SUBJECT PRONOUNS

I	*[ee-oh]*	**io**
You (informal, singular)	*[too]*	**tu**
You (formal, singular)	*[leh-ee]*	**lei**
He	*[eh-lyh]*	**egli**
She	*[ehl-lah]*	**ella**
They (masculine)	*[ehs-sih]*	**essi**
They (feminine)	*[ehs-seh]*	**esse**
We (masculine) We (feminine)	*[noh-ee]*	**noi**
you (formal and informal, plural.)	*[voh-ee]*	**voi**

You'll notice that, in Italy, there are a lot more subject pronouns than in English! Aside from *who* they reference, they're also split up based on:

➲ Formality of the situation.

➲ Genders of the people you're talking about.

➲ Quantity of subjects, i.e., whether you're just talking to or about one person or more.

Unlike English, there are different Italian pronouns for 'you' and 'they' depending on how many people you're talking to or talking about. Saying *voi* would be like the equivalent of saying 'you all' or 'both of you.'

Let's get familiar with these pronouns, shall we?

1.1. Practice

A. Translate the following pronouns:

1.   We (feminine): _____

2.   I: _____

3.   They feminine: _____

4.   They plural: _____

5.   You (informal plural in Italy): _____

6.   You (informal singular): _____

7.   You (formal and informal plural in Italy): _____

8.   We (masculine): _____

B. Write the correct subject pronoun:

1.   _____ vengo a casa tua (*I'm going to your house*).

2.   _____ siamo tuoi amici (*we—masculine—are your friends*).

3.   _____ siete i migliori (*you—masculine informal plural in Italy—are the best*)

4.   _____ siete uomini (*you— formal and informal plural in Italy—are men*).

5.   _____ sono amici (*they—masculine—are friends*).

6.   _____ sei una donna (*you—singular informal— are a woman*).

C. Replace the names between parentheses with an adequate pronoun:

1.   (Paolo)_____ e (Maria) _____ si sposeranno (*will get married*).

2.   (They) _____ si sposeranno (*will get married*) in una chiesa (in a church).

3.   (You/masculine/plural/informal Italy)_____ siete invitati al matrimonio (*are invited to the wedding*).

4. _____ (Luisa and you/informal), volete andare al matrimonio? (*want to go to the wedding?*)

5. (Tommaso and I)_____ abbiamo una sorpresa (*have a surprise*) per (they/

   masculine)_____.

6. (Pietro) _____ vive in Messico (lives in México).

7. (Julia) _____ vive in Ecuador (lives in Ecuador).

The Difference Between Formal (*Lei*) and Informal (*tu*) Pronouns

Earlier, we briefly touched on how different pronouns are used based on the formality of a situation. For example, if you were speaking directly to one person ('you'), you'd use the word **tu** in an informal situation and **Lei** in a formal situation. But what exactly constitutes an informal or formal situation?

You'd use the formal word **Lei** in interactions with people like:

- Your boss

- A stranger or new acquaintance (unless you dislike them and want them to know it!)

- A salesperson

- The cashier at the bank

You'd use the informal pronoun **tu** with:

- Your friends
- Your family
- Children and animals

- People you intend to insult
- Other young people (if you're young, too)

What if you're not sure whether to use *tu* or *Lei*?

Situations may arise where you're not sure whether to go with the informal or formal pronoun. In this case, be safe and go with the formal ***Lei***! It's much better to be overly polite than to risk coming across as rude or insulting

> The masculine plural form **essi** refers to a group of males or to a group that includes both males and females. The feminine plural form **esse** only refers to a group of females. In other words, the default word for 'They' is **essi**, unless you're referring to a group of people that's entirely female.

INTERESTING FACT

In Italian, there is no subject pronoun **it**. You use **egli** and **ella** to refer to people, and sometimes animals. You don't use **egli** and **ella** to refer to things. It would be like calling a shoe or a potato 'he' and 'she.' Quirky, but not exactly accurate!

1.2. Practice

A. What would you say with each of the following, **tu** or **lei**?

1.   Your grandmother _____

2.   A co-worker _____

3.   A flight attendant _____

4.   Your boss _____

5.   A little boy _____

6.   A professor _____

7.   A repair person _____

8.   Your cousin _____

9.   Your best friend _____

10.   Your father-in-law _____

B. Say which pronoun you would use according to the situation: **tu/voi**

1. You ask the waiter at a restaurant in Italian when your table will be ready. He answers:
    _____ siete i prossimi (*you're up next*).

2. You ask your friends in Italy if they want to come with you to the park: _____ volete venire
    con me? (*Do you want to come with me?*)

3. You tell your friends in Italian that they're your best friends: _____

4. _____ siete i miei migliori amici (*You are my best friends*).

5. You tell your friends in Italy they are the best Instagram followers you could have: _____
    siete i migliori follower su Instagram che possa avere1 (*You are the best Instagram followers I could
    have*).

6. You tell your friends in Italian: "You guys are the best followers that a YouTuber could have":
    _____ siete i migliori follower che un YouTuber possa avere (*You are the best followers a
    YouTuber could have*).

7. You tell your friend in Italian: "_____ sai cucinare molto bene." (*You know how to cook very
    well*).

2 GREETINGS AND EXPRESSIONS OF POLITENESS

As we mentioned earlier, your word choices will vary depending on the formality of the situation. This
applies to pronouns, and it also applies to longer exchanges, like greetings. In English, formality and
informality matters too! For example, you probably wouldn't enter a formal meeting with your boss and say,
"Hey, what's up?"

In Italian, it's no different. You'll have different greetings for different types of situations. The words might
mean essentially the same thing, but the choices convey whether you're familiar or unfamiliar with the

person or people you're addressing.

Informal Greeting

Consider the following informal greeting between Maria and Pedro, two young housemates that go to the same college. Since they're both peers, they'll use informal language with each other, even if they're not that close.

Maria: Ciao, Pietro. (*Hi, Pedro*)

Pietro: Ciao, Maria. Come va? (*Hi, Maria. How's it going?*)

Maria: Bene. E tu? (*Good. And you?*)

Pietro: Molto bene! A dopo. (*Very good! See you later*)

Maria: Ci vediamo. (*Bye*)

Formal Greeting

Now, let's look at a formal greeting between il signor Pérez and la signorina Alonso. Il signor Pérez is a security guard at signorina Alonso's apartment building. Even though they're both middle-aged, they would use formal language with each other since they don't know each other well and they aren't exactly peers.

Signor Pérez: Buon pomeriggio, signorina Alonso. (*Good afternoon*, signorina Alonso)

Signorina Alonso: Buon pomeriggio, signor Pérez. Come sta? (*Good afternoon*, Signor Pérez. How are you?)

Signor Pérez: Molto bene, grazie. E lei? (*Very good, thank you. And you?*)

Signorina Alonso: Molto bene, grazie. Arrivederci. (*Very good, thanks. Goodbye*)

Signor Pérez: A presto. (*See you later*)

Both the informal and formal greetings essentially say the same thing, but they'll use different words in the formal exchange to express politeness. That said, some words and phrases will remain the same. You can still say **bene** or **molto bene** to say you're doing well or very well, and in either situation, you'll still say **arrivederci** to say goodbye.

Vocabulary: greetings

Ciao	[chee-ah-oh]	Hi
Come va?	[coh-meh vah]	How's it going?
Bene	[beh-neh]	Good
E tu?	[he too]	And you?
Molto bene	[mohl-toh beh-neh]	Very good
A dopo	[ah doh-poh]	See you later
Arrivederci	[ahr-ree-veh-dehr-chee]	Goodbye
Ciao	[chee-ah-oh]	Bye

Come va?, **Come stai?**, and **E tu?** are greeting expressions used in informal situations, with people you know well, on a first-name basis.

Vocabulary: more greetings

Buongiorno	[bwon-johr-noh]	Good morning
Buon pomeriggio	[bwon poh-meh-ree-joh]	Good afternoon
Buonanotte	[bwoh-nah-noht-teh]	Good evening, good night
Signor (Sig.)	[see-nyohr]	Mr.
Signora (Sig.ra)	[see-nyoh-rah]	Mrs.
Signorina (Sig.na)	[see-nyoh-ree-nah]	Miss
Lei come sta?	[leh-ee koh-meh stah]	How are you?
E lei?	[eh leh-ee]	And you?
A dopo	[ah doh-poh]	See you later
A domani	[ah doh-mah-nee]	See you tomorrow

Come stai? and **E lei?** are used to address someone with whom you have a more formal relationship, like your boss or a salesperson.

3 LANGUAGE ETIQUETTE

Next are the "magic" words and phrases that will help you address others politely in everyday life. Say your please and thank you in Italian, just like you do in English.

grazie	[grah-tsee-eh]	thanks / thank you
molte grazie	[mohl-the grah-tsee-eh]	thanks a lot / thank you very much
di nulla	[dee nuhl-lah]	you're welcome
per favore	[pehr fah-voh-reh]	please
scusa	[skoo-zah]	excuse me / pardon me (to get someone's attention or to apologize to someone or for something you did)
con permesso/ permesso	[kohn pehr-mehs-soh]/ [pehr-mehs-soh	excuse me / pardon me (to ask for permission to go through a group of people)
Non è niente	[nohn eh nah-dah]	it's nothing
scusate	[skoo-zah-teh]	excuse me (to get someone's attention or to apologize to someone for something you did)

3.1. Practice

A. Choose the most appropriate response from the list on the right to the following greetings or expressions:

1. Molte grazie _____
2. Buongiorno _____
3. Scusa _____
4. Come va? _____
5. Arrivederci _____
6. Buon pomeriggio _____
7. Come sta? _____

A. Molto bene.
B. Bene, grazie, E lei?
C. Di niente
D. Buongiorno, come sta?
E. Non è niente
F. A dopo
G. Bene, E tu?

B. What might these people say to each other if they met or passed each other at the time given?

1. Laura and Mathew at 2.00 p.m.

2. Mary and her boss at 7.00 a.m.

3. You and your friend at 12.00 a.m.

4. Joe and Ann at 10.00 p.m.

5. You and your Math teacher at 11 a.m.

C. Match the situation with what you say if it happens

1. You accidentally bump into a person on the street.   Permesso

2. You're trying to squeeze your way out of a packed subway.   Non è niente

3. A waiter apologizes for spilling water on your shirt.   Scusate

4. You're trying to reach the aisle at the movie theatre   Scusa
    to use the restroom.   Di niente

5. You're trying to draw the cashier's attention at the supermarket,
    who's sitting with his back to you.

6. An elderly woman thanks you for helping her cross the street.

D. Choose the most appropriate response to the following statements or questions

1. Molte grazie   A dopo

2. Come va?   Non è niente

3. Come stai?   Bene, E tu?

4. Arrivederci   Molto bene, grazie

5. Scusate   Di niente

E. Complete the following dialogue with the right greeting or phrase.

YOU: Ciao, Martino, _____ [1] ?

MARTINO: Bene, grazie, _____ [2] ?

YOU: Molto _____ [3] .

MARTINO: Arrivederci. _____ [4] mattina.

YOU: _____ [5] .

Common Mistake:

Remember it's "Buongiorno," but "Buon pomeriggio" and "Buonanotte."

ANSWER KEY

Practice. 1.1

A.   1. noi 2. io 3. ella 4. egli 5. voi 6. tu 7. voi 8. noi

B.   1. io 2. noi 3. voi 4. voi 5. essi 6. tu

C.   1. lui e lei 2. essi 3. voi 4. voi 5. noi/essi 6. lui 7. ella

Practice. 1.2

A.   1. tu 2. tu 3. lei 4. lei 5. tu 6. lei 7. lei 8 tu 9. tu 10. lei

B.   1. voi 2. voi 3. voi 4. voi 5. voi 6. tu

Practice. 3.1

A. 1.c 2. d 3. e 4. g 5. f 6. a 7. b

B. 1. Buon pomeriggio 2. Buongiorno 3. Buon pomeriggio 4. Buonanotte 5. Buongiorno

C. 1. Scusate/Scusa 2. Permesso 3. Non è niente 4. Permesso 5. Scusate 6. Di niente

D. 1. Di niente 2. Bene, E tu? 3. Molto bene, grazie 4. A dopo5. Non è niente

E. 1. Come va? 2. E tu? 3. bene 4. A presto 5. Arrivederci

We invite you to scan this **QR code** using the camera of your phone to access your bonus content:

SCAN THE QR CODE BELOW

Now that you are done with lesson 1, as a reward we give you access to the **audiobook version** that will help you to improve your pronunciation and enrich your vocabulary.

You will also find **complementary 2 eBOOKs** with the best tips for traveling abroad, and more...

LESSON 02

THE DOG AND A CAT

NOUNS AND ARTICLES

1 THE GENDER OF NOUNS AND THE SINGULAR DEFINITE ARTICLE

We covered pronouns, but what's a noun? Nouns are objects, places, and things.

In Italian, nouns are called **sustantivos**, but don't worry you don't need to remember this just yet. Unlike English, all nouns in Italian are either masculine or feminine. This doesn't mean that objects are perceived as having literal gender differences, of course, but rather, they are just classified into different groups.

Some of these are straightforward, such as **l'uomo** and **la donna,** which mean *the man* and *the woman* respectively. As you'd expect, **l'uomo** is a masculine noun and **la donna** is a feminine noun. Although they're different words, **il** and **la** both mean 'the' – they simply apply to different genders. You would never ever say 'la uomo' or 'il donna' as it would be grammatically incorrect.

It's easy with people, but less easy with objects and places. To speak fluent Italian, you'll need to get used to the genders of different nouns. For example, you'll need to remember that a book is masculine while a photograph is feminine.

The definite article (the) should always agree with the gender of the noun. This is a hard one for English speakers, because we only have one definite article—the—and don't have to worry about the rest!

Singular Masculine Nouns

So, is there a way to tell masculine from feminine nouns? Well, most masculine nouns end in **-o**.

As we mentioned earlier, the masculine singular noun uses the definite article **il**. This shows we are referring to just one of the thing, place, or objects we are referring to. Don't worry about plural nouns for now, we'll get to those later.

l'uomo	[lwoh-moh]	*the man*
l'amico	[lah-mee-koh]	*the friend (male)*
il ragazzo	[eel rah-gaht-tsoh]	*the boy*
il figlio	[eel fee-lyoh]	*the son*
il fratello	[eel frha-tehl-loh]	*the brother*
il nonno	[eel nohn-noh]	*the grandfather*
lo zio	[loh tsee-oh]	*the uncle*
il gatto	[eel gaht-toh]	*the cat*

The dog and a cat

il pomodoro	[eel poh-moh-doh-roh]	*the tomato*
il libro	[eel lee-broh]	*the book*
il telefono	[eel teh-leh-foh-noh]	*the telephone*
il giovane	[eel joh-vah-neh]	*the youngster*

Some masculine nouns end in -e:

il caffè	[eel kahf-feh]	*the coffee*
lo studente	[loh stuh-dehn-teh]	*the student*
il cane	[eel kah-neh]	*the dog*

Alright, so not *all* masculine nouns end in -o. Most of them do, but there are some exceptions. Here are some masculine nouns that end in **-a** or **-ma**. Regardless of how the word ends, you'll still need to use **il** if it's masculine.

il clima	[eehl klee-mah]	*the climate*
il programma	[eehl proh-grahm-mah]	*the program*
il sistema*	[eehl see-steh-mah]	*the system*
la mappa	[lah mahp-pah]	*the map*
la lingua	[lah leen-gwah]	*the language*
il pianeta	[eehl pee-ah-neh-tah]	*the planet*

The dog and a cat

il problema	[eehl proh-bleh-mah]	*the problem*
il turista	[eehl too-ree-stah]	*the tourist*
il sofá	[eehl soh-fah]	*the sofa*

> **Be careful!** Many English speakers say "la sistema," thinking this word is feminine. Remember, it's "**il sistema**."

TIP

Since there is no clear rule about what ending a noun should have to be masculine, you'll need to memorize which noun is what gender. Don't worry, this gets easier with practice!

Singular Feminine Nouns

On the other hand, feminine nouns usually end in **-a**. The feminine singular noun uses the definite article **la**.

la persona	[lah pehr-soh-nah]	*the person*
la donna	[lah dohn-nah]	*the woman*
la madre	[lah mah-dreh]	*the mother*
la amica	[lah ah-mee-kah]	*the friend (female)*

la bambina	[lah bahm-bee-nah]	the girl
la ragazza	[lah rah-gaht-tsah]	the girl
la figlia	[lah fee-lyah]	the daughter
la sorella	[lah soh-rehl-lah]	the sister
la nonna	[lah nohn-nah]	the grandmother
la zia	[lah tsee-ah]	the aunt
la gatta	[lah gaht-tah]	the cat (female)
la cagna	[lah kah-nyah]	the dog (female)
la casa	[lah kah-sah]	the house
la pietanza	[lah koh-mee-dah]	the food
la sedia	[lah seh-deeah]	the chair

Some feminine nouns end in **-zione, -sione, -tà, -cia, or -zia**.

la conversazione	[lah kohn-vehr-sah-tsyoh-neh]	the conversation
la televisione	[lah teh-leh-vee-syoh-neh]	the television
la verità	[lah veh-ree-tah]	the truth
la città	[lah cheet-tah]	the city

The dog and a cat

| la farmacia | [lah fahr-mah-chee-ah] | *The drugstore* |
| l'amicizia | [lah-mee-chee-tsyah] | *the friendship* |

And even some feminine nouns end in **-o**!

la foto	[lah foh-toh]	*the photograph*
la mano	[lah mah-noh]	*the hand*
la radio	[lah rah-dyoh]	*the radio*
la moto	[lah moh-toh]	*the motorcycle*

Again, since many feminine nouns don't follow a regular pattern, you need to learn each noun with its article, so you don't make mistakes like saying, "il mano," when it should be "**la mano**."

1.1. Practice

What's the appropriate masculine or feminine form of the definite article (the) for each noun? And while you're at it, try translating the word to see if you remember the meaning!

1. _____ foto
2. _____ ospedale
3. _____ televisore
4. _____ casa
5. _____ libro

6. _____ città
7. _____ conversazione
8. _____ figlio
9. _____ pianeta
10. _____ amico

B.

1. _____ mappa
2. _____ programma
3. _____ sistema
4. _____ problema
5. _____ hotel

6. _____ persona
7. _____ animale
8. _____ cibo
9. _____ mano
10. _____ telefono

── Common Mistake: ──

The noun **delta** (*esthuary of a river*) ends in **-a** but is masculine: **il delta** (*the delta*). So don't say, **la delta**!

---

2 PLURAL NOUNS AND THE PLURAL DEFINITE ARTICLE

Plural Nouns

So far, we've only covered singular nouns. That is, just one object, place, or thing. But what if you wanted to refer to multiple friends, not just one friend? Or many books, not just a single book? This is where plural nouns come in.

In English, we usually indicate that there is *more* than one thing by adding "s" to the end of the word, like 'friends' or 'books.' In Italian, plurality is also indicated by modifying the ending of the word.

For Italian male nouns, that ends in **-o** (amico - *friend*) or **-e** (studente - *student*), the plural form is **-i** (amic**i**, studen**ti**). If you're referring to more than one friend, you would then use the word **amici**, and for more than one student, you would use **studenti.**

Hopefully, you're getting the hang of this by now! If you're referring to multiple pencils, you'd use the word **matite.** And for multiple noses, you would use the word **narici**.

You might notice that something is missing – the definite article. How do we say 'the tables' or 'the cities?

Just like the nouns, the definite articles are also modified to indicate plurality. We must also keep in mind the gender of the noun!

The masculine definite article **il/lo** becomes **i/gli.**

The feminine definite article **la** becomes **le.**

For example...

L'amico → gli amici

La casa → le case

In some cases, the plural form is indicated by the article, whereas the noun does not change. For example:

la città (*singular – the city*) **le** città (*plural – the cities*)

Remember that in Italian, if we're referring to multiple people that consist of both females and males, we use the masculine plurality by default. So, you would use the term **gli amici** when referring to your friends if your friends include female and male people.

To clarify...

Gli amici = male friends OR male friends + female friends

Keep in mind that, just like in English, we don't always need to use the definite article. In English, the definite article is the word 'the,' and in Italian, this is **il/lo, la, i/gli,** and **le.** So, when do you need to use the definite article?

First, let's just quickly go over what the point of the definite article is. Let's use an English example.

If you have a salad in your fridge that you really need to eat before it goes bad, you would say 'I need to eat *the* salad.' Using the definite article indicates that you have a specific salad in mind. It's already there and it's just waiting to be eaten!

However, if you feel like you've been eating too much fast food lately, you might say 'I need to eat *a* salad.' In this case, you don't have a specific salad in mind, you just need to eat any salad. That's why we call it the *definite* article because there is more certainty and specificity implied.

These rules about when to use the definite article also apply to Italian – but a couple of extra ones are added on top. Let's summarize!

In Italian, the definite article (**il/lo, la, gli, le**) is used...

➲ Like English, to refer to a specific thing person or thing. **La donna di Adamo** è **Eva** (*Eve is Adam's woman*).

➲ Unlike English, to refer to something in a conceptual or broad sense. **Mi piace la carne** (*I like meat*) or **mi piace la musica** (*I like music*)

➲ Unlike English, to refer to parts of your own body. **Mi hai rotto il braccio** (*I broke my arm*)

In Italian with the nouns starting with a vowel, the article "loses" the vowel, due to the encounter of two vowels. It always happens. **Always**.

Examples:

l'arte (*the art*) instead of la arte; **l'amico**, instead of "lo amico"; **l'incontro** (*the encounter*) instead of "lo incontro"; **l'uomo** (*the man*) instead of "lo uomo".

2.1.   Practice

Write the plural version of each singular noun. When you finish, read each pair out loud.

1. L'uomo _____

2. L'amica _____

3. La conversazione _____

4. L'animale _____

5. Il sistema _____

6. Il bambino _____

7. La casa _____

8. Il treno _____

9. La città _____

10. Il dottore _____

B. Write the singular version of each plural noun. When you finish, read each pair out loud.

1. Le verità _____
2. Le televisioni _____
3. Le mani _____
4. Le cagne _____

5. Le matite _____
6. Le bambine _____
7. Le radio _____
8. Le cene _____

3 THE INDEFINITE ARTICLE

So, we've already talked about the definite article. What about the indefinite article? Remember when we talked about the difference between 'I need to eat *the* salad' and 'I need to eat *a* salad'? As you can probably guess, it's in '*a* salad' where the indefinite article is used. We use the indefinite article to refer to a thing that is non-specific.

In English, the indefinite article is *a* or *an*. In Italian, the indefinite articles are...

Masculine/Neutral, singular: **un/uno** (*a/an*)

Masculine, plural: **alcuni** (*some*)

Feminine, singular: **una** (*a/an*)

Feminine, plural: **alcune** (*some*)

For example:

Un'amica (*a female friend*) → **alcune amiche** (*some female friends*)

Un figlio (*a son*) → **alcuni figli** (*some sons*)

To summarize, you only use the indefinite article (**un/uno, alcuni, una, alcune**) when:

➲ You want to identify someone or something as part of a class or group: è **un animale** (*it's an animal*).

➲ You want to refer to something in a non-specific way: **una barca** è **per navigare** (*a boat is for sailing*) or è **una donna giovane** (*She's a young woman*).

Quick Recap

	MASCULINE SINGULAR NOUNS	MASCULINE PLURAL NOUNS	FEMININE SINGULAR NOUNS	FEMININE PLURAL NOUNS
DEFINITE ARTICLES	**l'**amico (the male friend)	**gli** amici (the male friends)	**l'**amica (the female friend)	**le** amiche (the female friends)
INDEFINITE ARTICLES	**un** amico (a male friend)	**alcuni** amici (some male friends or some female and male friends)	**un'**amica (a female friend)	**alcune** amiche (some female friends)

Un and **una** (*a and an*) can mean *one* as well as *a* or *an*. You will understand which one it means based on the context. For example, **Un** bambino (*a boy*) vs. Compro **un** pomodoro (*I buy one tomato*).

Speak Abroad
Academy

3.1. Practice

A. Turn these singular nouns with indefinite articles into plural nouns with their indefinite articles.

1.   un nonno _____

2.   una conversazione: _____

3.   un cane: _____

4.   una donna: _____

5.   uno studente: _____

6.   un dottore: _____

7.   un hotel: _____

8.   un treno: _____

9.   una matita: _____

10. una città: _____

B. Translate the following:

1.   The (male and female) students: _____

2.   The planets _____

3.   A (female) doctor _____

4.   Some photographs _____

5.   The language _____

6.   The tourists _____

7.   Some (male and female) friends _____

8.   A tomato _____

9.   The conversation _____

10. Some truths _____

C. Complete the sentences with **il/lo, la, i/gli, le** or **un/uno, una, alcuni, alcune**

1.   _____ casa di Giovanni.

2.   Ho trovato (*I found*) _____ moneta (*coin*).

3.   È _____ testa (*head*) di _____ leone.

The dog and a cat

4. Quella è _____ impronta (*footprint*).

5. Sono _____ amiche di mia sorella (*they are some friends of my sisters*)

6. Mi piace _____ pollo (I like chicken).

7. Sto portando _____ torta a casa tua (*I'm taking a cake to your house*).

8. Pietro sta comprando _____ bevande per la festa (*Pedro is buying the drinks for the party*).

D. Do you remember what these nouns are in English? Remember to translate them with the definite or indefinite article that precedes them.

1. Il libro _____

2. La casa _____

3. I fiori _____

4. Il ragazzo _____

5. I fratelli _____

6. Il caffè _____

7. Il treno _____

8. I pianeti _____

9. Un gatto _____

10. Alcuni cani _____

11. Il telefono _____

12. Le mani _____

13. Un programma _____

14. Alcuni sistemi _____

15. I libri _____

16. La città _____

E. Circle the right answer:

1. la/una _____ madre di Tommaso è simpatica.

2. Vorrei _____ i/alcuni libri da leggere.

3. Vorrei _____ il/un televisore nuovo.

4. _____ il/un gatto è un animale independente.

5. Ha rotto (*he broke*) _____ la/una finestra della casa.

6. Mi piacciono _____ i/alcuni fiori.

7. Ho parlato (*I spoke*) con _____ il/un direttore del collegio.

8.   Teresa ha trovato _____ el/un gatto.

9.   Ho messo (*I put*) _____ le/alcune chiavi (*keys*) nella borsetta (*purse*).

F. Complete these sentences with the right definite or indefinite article (**il-lo/la/i-gli/le/un-uno/una/ alcuni/alcune**)

1.   Washington è _____ città degli Stati Uniti.

2.   Hudson è _____ via di casa tua.

3.   Bogotá è _____ capitale della Colombia.

4.   _____ casa di Elena è grande.

5.   _____ Papa vive a Roma.

6.   Ho bisogno (*I need*) _____ giacca (*jacket*) rossa.

7.   Hai _____ chiavi (*keys*) di casa?

8.   Ho visto (*I saw*) _____ leone (*lion*) grande allo zoo (*zoo*).

ANSWER KEY

Practice. 1.1

A.   1. la 2. il 3. la 4. la 5. il 6. la 7. la 8. il 9. il 10. il

B.   11. il 12. il 13. il 14. il 15. il 16. la 17. il 18. la 19. la 20. il

Practice. 2.1

A.   1. gli uomini 2. le amiche 3. le conversazioni 4. gli animali 5. i sistemi 6. i bambini 7. le case 8. i treni
     9. le città 10. i dottori

B.   1. la verità 2. il televisore 3. la mano 4. la cagna 5. la matita 6. la bambina 7. la radio 8. il cibo

Practice. 3.1

A.   1. alcuni nonni 2. alcune conversazioni 3. alcuni cani 4. alcune donne 5. alcuni studenti 6. alcuni dottori 7. alcuni hotel 8. alcuni treni 9. alcune matite 10. alcune città

B.   1. gli studenti 2. i pianeti 3. una dottoressa 4. alcune foto 5. l'idioma 6. i turisti 7. alcuni amici 8. un pomodoro 9. la conversazione 10. alcune verità

C.   1. la 2. una 3. la / un 4. una 5. alcune 6. il 7. un 8. le

D.   1. il libro 2. la casa 3. i fiori 4. il più giovane 5. i fratelli 6. il caffè 7. il treno 8. i pianeti 9. un gatto 10. alcuni cani 11. il telefono 12. le mani 13. un programma 14. alcuni sistemi 15. i libri 16. la città

E.   1. la 2. alcuni 3. una 4. il 5. una 6. le 7. il 8. un 9. le

F.   1. una 2. la 3. la 4. la 5. il 6. una 7. le 8. un

LESSON 03

BROWN DOG AND BLACK CAT

DESCRIBING PEOPLE AND THINGS

1 DESCRIPTIVE ADJECTIVES

Remember what a noun is? It's a person, place, or thing, like 'house' or 'table.'

Sometimes it isn't enough to simply mention the object or subject – sometimes, it's necessary to describe the object or subject. This is where adjectives come in. We use adjectives to describe the nouns we're talking about. For example, we could say that a person is fat or thin – or that a table is big or small.

In Italian, we usually put the adjective *after* the noun that we're describing.

So, to say 'big table,' this would look like **tavolo <u>grande</u>.** As you can guess, the word **grande** means big and it is the adjective.

Adjectives are also used to describe other qualities, like the nationality of something or someone. For example, to say 'Italian food,' we would say **cibo <u>italiano.</u>**

Although we usually put the adjective after the noun, there is one instance when we put the descriptor *before* the noun. And this is when we're describing the quantity of something. For example, when we say, 'few pencils,' this would be **<u>qualche</u> matita.**

Adjectives won't always have the same ending. They will depend on

Gender of the noun

⮐   The singularity or plurality of the noun

So, if you have a feminine singular noun like **la foto** (the photo), you will need to use a feminine singular adjective like **bell<u>a</u>** (beautiful) to describe it. In this case, you would say **la foto bell<u>a</u>** to say, 'the beautiful photo.'

Singular form of adjectives

Adjectives that end in **-o** are masculine and agree with a masculine noun. For example: L'amico **buono** (*the good friend*). Keep in mind that Italian adjectives are the last words in the sentence, since they usually go after the noun.

Lo studente alto	[loh stoo-dehn-teh ahl-toh	*The tall student*
Il bambino basso	[eel bahm-bee-noh bahs-soh]	*The short boy*
Il fratello buono	[eel frah-tehl-loh bwoh-noh]	*The good brother*
Il cane cattivo	[eel kah-neh kaht-tee-voh]	*The bad dog*

Il gatto grasso	[eel gaht-toh grahs-soh]	*The fat cat*
Lo zio magro	[loh tsee-oh mah-groh]	*The thin uncle*
Il bambino simpatico	[eel bahm-bee-noh seem-pah-tee-koh]	*The friendly boy*
Il ragazzo antipatico	[eel rah-gaht-tsoh ahn-tee-pah-tee-koh]	*The unfriendly youngster*
Il libro piccolo	[eel lee-broh peek-koh-loh]	*The small book*
Il nonno lavoratore	[eel nohn-noh lah-voh-rah-toh-reh]	*The hardworking grandfather*
Il sofa bellissimo	[eel soh-fah behl-lees-see-moh]	*The beautiful sofa*
L'uomo vecchio	[lwoh-moh vehk-kyo]	*The old man*
Il bambino dispettoso	[eel bahm-bee-no dee-speht-toh-soh]	*The mischievous boy*

But what if you're not referring to a masculine noun? Sometimes, you need to describe a female student is tall, not just a male student!

In this case, adjectives change the **-o** to **-a** when they describe a feminine noun. For example: La bambina **buona** (*the good girl*).

La studentessa alta	[lah stoo-dehn-tehs-sah ahl-tah]	*The tall (female) student*
La bambina bassa	[lah bahm-bee-nah bahs-sah]	*The short girl*
La sorella buona	[lah soh-rehl-lah bwoh-nah]	*The good sister*
La cagna cattiva	[lah kah-nya kaht-tee-vah]	*The bad (female) dog*

La gatta grassa	[lah gaht-tah grahs-sa]	*The fat (female) cat*
La zia magra	[lah tsee-ah mah-grah]	*The thin aunt*
La bambina simpatica	[lah bahm-bee-na seem-pah-tee-kah]	*The friendly girl*
La ragazza antipatica	[lah rah-gaht-tsa ahn-tee-pah-tee-kah]	*The unfriendly (female) youngster*
La casa piccola	[lah kah-sah peek-koh-lah]	*The small house*
La nonna lavoratrice	[lah nohn-nah lah-voh-rah-tree-cheh]	*The hardworking grandmother*
La città bellissima	[lah ceeht-ta behl-lees-see-mah]	*The beautiful city*
La donna vecchia	[lah dohn-nah vehk-kya]	*The old woman*

Sometimes, you don't need to change the ending of an adjective. This makes it a little easier!

If the adjective ends in **-e** (intelligente), they will have the same form whether they describe a feminine or masculine noun: uomo **fedele** (loyal man) and donna **fedele** (loyal woman).

Il libro eccellente	[eel leeh-broh ehch-chehl-lehn-teh]	*The excellent book*
L'uomo povero	[lwoh-moh poh-veh-roh]	*The poor man*
Il pianeta grande	[eel pee-ah-neh-tah grahn-deh]	*The big planet*
L'amico Fedele	[lah-mee-koh feh-deh-leh]	*The loyal friend*
Il bambino debole	[eel bahm-bee-noh deh-boh-leh]	*The weak boy*

La conversazione difficile	[lah kohn-vehr-sah-tyoh-neh]	*The difficult conversation*
Il tema facile	[eel the-mah fah-cheeh-leh]	*The easy issue*
La donna forte	[lah dohn-nah fohr-teh]	*The strong woman*
Il cibo eccellente	[eel chee-boh ehch-chehl-ehn-teh]	*The excellent food*
La signora gentile	[lah see-nyoh-rah jehn-tee-leh]	*The kind lady*
Lo studente giovane	[loh stoo-dehn-teh joh-vah-neh]	*The (male) young student*
La dottoressa intelligente	[lah doht-toh-rehs-sah een-tehl-lee-jehn-teh]	*The intelligent (female) doctor*
La bambina allegra	[lah bahm-bee-nah ahl-leh-grah]	*The cheerful girl*

Now, let's introduce another rule.

Remember when I said that the Italian adjective *usually* goes after the noun? If you want to emphasize the quality of something or add an emotional charge to a description, you can sometimes place the adjective before the noun. In this case, the adjective will be shortened.

For example, **buono** and **grande** may all appear before the noun. When **buono** and **grande** precede a masculine singular noun, **buono** will become **buon** and **grande** will become **gran.**

Un libro buono and **un buon libro** both mean *'a good book,'* but you may choose to say **un buon libro** to emphasize just how much you enjoyed this excellent book.

On the other hand, if you thought a program was particularly bad, you might choose to say **un brutto programma** instead of **un programma brutto.** They both mean 'a bad program,' but the former places more of an emotional charge on the word 'bad.'

Brown dog and black cat

Sometimes, this can slightly change the meaning of the adjectives in question.

When **grande** is placed after a noun, it simply means large or big, like in the sentence **una casa grande** (*a large house*). When it is placed before a singular noun instead of after, it is shortened to **gran** and means impressive or great. You could even say **un gran dottore** to say, 'a great doctor.'

1.2.   Practice

A. Translate the English adjective into its Italian equivalent. Make sure it matches the noun.

1.   La bambina _____(tall)

2.   L'uomo _____ (poor)

3.   Il cane _____ (loyal)

4.   La ragazza _____ (beautiful)

5.   Il problema _____ (difficult)

6.   Il bambino _____ (good)

7.   Il nonno _____ (happy)

8.   Il libro _____ (interesting)

9.   L'amicizia _____ (strong)

10.   La mano _____ (weak)

B. Translate the English adjective into its Italian equivalent. Make sure it matches the noun.

1.   La zia _____ (short)

2.   Il cibo _____ (excellent)

3.   La città _____ (small)

4.   Lo zio _____ (friendly)

5.   L'hotel _____ (old)

6.   Il gatto _____ (bad)

7.   L'amica _____ (intelligent)

8.   La cagna _____ (loyal)

9.   Il ragazzo _____ (hardworking)

10.   Il turista _____ (fat)

C. Write the opposite adjectives to the one in the sentences below.

1.   Il tema facile _____

2.   Il bambino basso _____

3.   Il ristorante cattivo _____

4.   La bambina antipatica _____

5.   Il cane piccolo _____

6.   L'uomo forte _____

Plural Form of Adjectives

_____
_____

I'm sure you guessed that this was coming! When the noun is plural and refers to multiple things, the adjectives must be modified to agree with the plurality.

1.3. Practice

A. Write the plural form of each of the following nouns and adjectives.

1.   Il pomodoro grande _____

2.   L'uomo alto _____

3.   Il cane intelligente _____

4.   La bambina forte _____

5.   La persona lavoratrice _____

6.   La città piccola _____

7.   Il gatto magro _____

8.   La donna allegra _____

9.   Il libro difficile _____

10.   Il cibo eccellente _____

B. Complete the sentence with the correct form of the adjectives:

1.   I libri _____ (eccellente)

2.   La nonna _____ (lavoratrice)

3.   La città _____ (bello)

4.   I libri _____ (piccolo)

5.   I sofà _____ (bello)

6.   Le sorelle _____ (buono)

7.   I gatti _____ (grasso)

8.   I bambini _____ (simpatico)

Brown dog and black cat

2 ADJECTIVES OF NATIONALITY

As we mentioned earlier, nationalities are also adjectives. They describe the quality of a thing or person. In Italian, the word for a country's language is sometimes the same as the word for the singular form of their nationality.

For example: **l'inglese** (English), **l'italiano** (Italian), and **il francese** (French).

This is similar to English, where the language 'English' uses the same word as the nationality 'English.' The same goes for 'Italiano' and 'French.'

In the Italian examples above, you'll notice that all three languages/nationalities are masculine. This means that the words for language and nationality are only interchangeable when the noun is masculine. When the noun is feminine, however, the adjective (in this case, the nationality) must be modified to a feminine form.

This means that you would say **lei è <u>francese</u>** (she is French) when you're talking about a female French person.

But if you were talking about a male French person, you could say **lui** è **<u>francese,</u>** using the same word for the language itself.

spagnolo	[spah-nyoh-loh]	*Spanish*
Inglese	[een-gleh-seh]	*English*
francese	[frahn-cheh-seh]	*French*
tedesco	[teh-deh-skoh]	*German*
italiano	[ee-tah-lyah-noh]	*Italian*

portoghese	[pohr-toh-geh-seh]	*Portuguese*
nordamericano	[nohrd-ah-meh-ree-kah-noh]	*Northamerican/American*

TIP

In Italian, you do not capitalize the names of languages and adjectives of nationality, though you do capitalize the names of countries and cities.

2.1. Practice

A. Write the nationality next to each noun, making it match in gender and number.

1. La Statua della Libertà è _____.

2. La Torre Eiffel è _____.

3. Il Big Ben è _____.

4. La Torre di Pisa è _____.

5. Il Museo El Prado è _____.

6. Angela Merkel è _____.

3   DESCRIBING A PERSON

In Italian, there's more than one way to write a descriptive sentence – just like in English. You can say 'the intelligent woman' or you can say 'the woman is intelligent.'

So far, we've only discussed how to say, 'the intelligent woman,' i.e. **la donna intelligente.** Now, let's try a different way of using these descriptors.

Brown dog and black cat

To say someone or something *is* something, you use the Italian word **è.** This means that 'the woman is intelligent' would become '**la donna** è **intelligente**.'

Of course, you don't always have to specify 'the woman,' you can also use pronouns to indicate who you're talking about. In this case, just replace the noun with the pronoun. To simply say 'she is intelligent,' you translate this to '**lei** è **intelligente.'**

Fortunately, the words 'is' and è are only different by one letter, so this should be somewhat easy to remember! You'll also be glad to hear that you use the word è no matter if you're talking about a feminine or masculine noun. For example, 'he is friendly' would be 'lui è **simpatico**.'

3.1.   Practice

A. Which adjectives are the most appropriate for each sentence?

1.   La zia Maria è _____ (bassi / intelligente / bella/ forti)

2.   Il signor García è _____ (lavoratrice / allegro / interessante / poveri)

3.   La città è _____ (grande / interessante / vecchio / bello)

4.   Il bambino è _____ (cattivi / buono / magra / simpatico)

5.   I gatti sono _____ (buono / cattivi / bianchi / nero

6.   I cani sono _____ (simpatici / allegri / fuerte / intelligente

B. Using the word è, choose two adjectives to describe the following people/things:

Adjectives

grande

pulita

1.   Mio padre è _____   simpatico

2.   Mia madre è _____   grasso

3.   Mio fratello è _____   lavoratrice

4.   Il mio gatto è _____   buono

5.   Il mio cane è _____   interessante

6.   La mia città è _____   bello

C. Translate the following:

1.   Monique is French: Monique è _____

2.   Carlo is Italian: Carlo è _____

3.   Helmut is German: Helmut è _____

4.   Sofía is Spanish: Sofia è _____

5.   María is Portuguese: Maria è _____

6.   Ted is English: Ted è _____

D. Do you remember where these famous people are from?

1.   Pablo Picasso è _____

2.   Emmanuel Macron è _____

3.   Daniel Craig è _____

4.   Marco Polo è _____

5.   Antonio Banderas è _____

6.   Miley Cyrus è _____

Common Error:

Remember not to make the mistake of placing the adjectives before the subject when you speak Italian.

Don't say Un **difficile** esame (*a difficult exam*) X when it should be: Un esame **difficile**! ✓

ANSWER KEY

Practice. 1.1

A.   1. alta 2. povero 3. fedele 4. bella 5. difficile 6. buono 7. felices 8. interessante 9. forte 10. debole

B.   6. bassa 7. eccellente 8. piccola 9. simpatico 10. vecchio 11. cattivo 12. intelligente 13. fedele 14 lavoratore 15. grasso

C.   1. Il tema difficile 2. Il bambino alto 3. Il ristorante buono 4. La bambina simpatica 5. Il cane grande 6. L'uomo debole

Practice. 1.2

A.   1. i pomodori grandi 2. gli uomini alti 3. i cani intelligenti 4. le bambine forti 5. le persone lavoratrici 6. le città piccole 7. i gatti magri 8. le donne allegre 9. i libri difficili 10. i cibi eccellenti

B.   1. eccellenti 2. lavoratrice 3. bella 4. piccoli 5. belli 6. buone 7. grassi 8. simpatici

Practice. 2.1

A.   1. nordamericana 2. francese 3. inglese 4. italiana 5. spagnola 6. tedesca

Practice. 3.1

A. 1. intelligente - bella 2. allegro - interessante 3. grande - interessante 4. buono - simpatico 5. cattivi - bianchi 6. simpatici - allegri

B. 1. buono, interessante, simpatico 2. interessante, lavoratrice 3. grasso, interessante, simpatico, bello, buono, grande 4. grande, simpatico, grasso, buono, bello 5. grande, simpatico, grasso, buono, bello 6. grande e pulita

C. 1. francese 2. italiano 3. tedesco 4. spagnola 5. portoghese 6. inglese

D. 1. spagnolo 2. francese 3. inglese 4. italiano 5. spagnolo 6. nordamericana

LESSON 04

THE YELLOW BRICK ROAD

DESCRIBING THINGS

1 MORE ADJECTIVES

Enough rules for now! It's time to learn some new words and just focus on expanding your vocabulary. By learning more Italian adjectives, you'll be able to describe the world, the people around you, and the experiences you have in greater detail.

Here are some useful everyday adjectives that you'll need to know!

Descriptive Adjectives

veloce	[veh-loh-cheh]	*fast*
lento	[lehn-toh]	*slow*
economico	[eh-koh-noh-mee-koh]	*cheap*
caro	[kah-roh]	*expensive*
famoso	[fah-moh-soh]	*famous*
lungo	[loohn-goh]	*long*
corto	[kohr-toh]	*short*
giovane	[joh-vah-neh]	*young*
anziano	[ahn-tsyag-noh]	*elderly*
carino	[kah-ree-noh]	*pretty*
brutto	[bruht-toh]	*ugly*
felice	[feh-lee-cheh]	*happy*
triste	[trees-teh]	*sad*
ricco	[reek-koh]	*rich*
nuovo	[nwoh-voh]	*new*

biondo	[byohn-doh]	*blond*
moro	[moh-roh]	*dark-haired / dark-skinned*
delizioso	[deh-leet-tsyoh-soh]	*delicious*

What do these adjectives look like in a sentence? Let's use them with some nouns we used in prior chapters.

Il problema facile (*the easy problem*)

La moto veloce (*the fast motorcycle*)

La sedia economica (*the cheap chair*)

La bambina famosa (*the famous girl*)

La donna felice (*the happy woman*)

L'uomo triste (*the sad man*)

Il bambino moro (*the dark-skinned boy*)

Il cibo delizioso (*the delicious food*)

La lezione breve (*the short lesson*)

Il treno lungo (*the long train*)

Colours

Of course, colours are adjectives too – and they're extremely important ones. All the rules you've learned about adjectives so far also apply to colours. Treat them just like you would all the other adjectives you've learned and place them after the noun.

bianco	[byahn-koh]	*white*
nero	[neh-roh]	*black*
rosso	[rohs-soh]	*red*
blu	[bluh]	*blue*
giallo	[jahl-loh]	*yellow*
verde	[vehr-deh]	*green*
grigio	[gree-joh]	*grey*
rosa/rosato	[roh-sah roh-sah-to]	*pink*
marrone	[mahr-roh-neh]	*brown*
arancione	[ah-rahn-chee-oh-neh]	*orange*

And here are some examples on how to use colours with a noun:

Il pianeta rosso (*the red planet*)

La matita nera (*the black pencil*)

The yellow brick road

Il gatto bianco (*the white cat*)

Il divano giallo (*the yellow sofa*)

La sedia verde (*the green chair*)

La moto blu (*the blue motorcycle*)

La casa rosa (*the pink house*)

La cagna marrone (*the brown dog*)

To modify these colours for plurality or multiple nouns, use the plural form (example: il cavallo nero – i cavalli neri) to the end of each adjective, except blue and pink that remain unchanged (example: la parete rosa – le pareti rosa). For example:

I pianeti rossi (*the red planets*)

Le matite nere (*the black pencils*)

I gatti bianchi (*the white cats*)

I sofà gialli (*the yellow sofa*)

Le sedie verdi (*the green chairs*)

Le moto blu (*the blue motorcycles*)

Le case rosa (*the pink houses*)

Le cagne marroni (*the brown dogs*)

1.1. Practice

A. Let's practice nouns

It's a good idea to practice what you already know so far: nouns (Second Lesson) and adjectives (Third Lesson and Fourth Lesson).

Find the right adjective for the following nouns according to the noun being masculine or feminine.

lavoratrice – cara – interessante – moro – difficile – veloce – felice – intelligente – vecchia – nuovo – fedele – alto – ricco – nuova – facile – economica – anziana – delizioso – marrone

1. La cagna è _____.
2. Il sofà e _____.
3. La ragazza è _____.
4. Il treno è _____.
5. Il bambino è _____.
6. Il televisore è _____.
7. Il caffè è _____.
8. La persona è _____.
9. La casa è _____.
10. La nonna è _____.
11. Il problema è _____.
12. La bambina è _____.
13. Il programma è _____.
14. L'uomo è _____.
15. La moto è _____.
16. La sedia è _____.
17. L'idioma è _____.
18. Il pomodoro è _____.

B. And now let's practice colours!

Complete the following phrases translating the colour adjectives from English to Italian.

1. Il fiore _____ (yellow)
2. La casa _____ (blue)
3. La sedia _____ (orange)
4. La mano _____ (white)
5. La gatta _____ (black)
6. La matita _____ (gris)

The yellow brick road

7.   Il sofá _____ (green)   9.   Il cane _____ (brown)

8.   Il telefono _____ (pink)   10. Il pomodoro _____ (red)

C. Answer these questions according to the example, by matching the adjectives to the noun.

Example: Il cane è intelligente. E i gatti? <u>Anche loro sono intelligenti</u>.

1.   La madre è gentile. E il padre? _____.

2.   L'esame di matematica è facile. E l'esame di letteratura? _____

3.   Le zie sono lavoratrici. E gli zii? _____

4.   Il cane è grasso. E i gatti? _____

5.   I nonni sono buoni. E la nonna? _____

6.   La sorella è forte. E i fratelli? _____

D.

1.   1. Elena and Sofía are quite opposite. What is Sofía like?

     Elena è bassa, fannullona, mora, triste e povera, invece Sofia è _____

     _____

2.   Tomás and Martín's house are the opposite. What is Martín's house like?

     La casa di Tommaso è piccola, bella, nuova, economica e alta, invece la casa di Martino è _____

     _____

3.   Germán and Pablo are quite opposite. What is Pablo like?

     Germano è ricco, intelligente, biondo, alto, lavoratore e vecchio, invece Paolo è_____

     _____

2 DEMONSTRATIVE ADJECTIVES

We've talked primarily about common adjectives so far. Now, let's talk about demonstrative adjectives. You've probably noticed that we're tossing around some very official linguistic terminology here. Let me just say that although it's important for you to be introduced to official terms like 'demonstrative adjective,' you don't have to remember them *if you remember the rule itself.*

So, let's talk about demonstrative adjectives.

These are words like 'this' or 'that,' which draw attention to specific nouns (singular or plural). You know what purpose they serve in English, and it's essentially the same in Italian.

When we use these words, they go *before* the noun, just like in English, and they also change if we're talking about multiple nouns. This is like the difference between 'this' and 'these.' For example, you would say **questo cane** for 'this dog' and **questi cani** for 'these dogs.'

And of course, they also need to be modified if you're talking about a feminine noun, like for example, **questa casa** (this house) and **queste case** (these houses).

this	**questo**	[kweh-stoh]	**questa**	[kweh-stah]
these	**questi**	[kweh-stee]	**queste**	[kweh-steh]
that	**quello**	[kwehl-loh]	**quella**	[kwehl-lah]
those	**quelli**	[kwehl-lee]	**quelle**	[kwehl-leh]

2.1. Practice

Beatriz and her friend go shopping. Check out what they say about the clothes, using the demonstrative adjective **questo** in the correct form. Use è (*is*) or **sono** (*are*) depending on whether the subject is singular or plural.

Example: vestito (dress) / rosso (red) → **Questo** vestito è rosso.

1. camicia (shirt) / bella → _____

2. scarpe (shoes) / care → _____

3. maglione (sweater) / lana (wool) → _____

4. vestiti (dresses) / seta (silk) → _____

5. pantaloni (pants) / economici _____

B. Now use the demonstrative adjective **quello** in the correct form.

Example: calze (socks) / lunghe → **Queste** calze sono lunghe.

1. casacca (*blouse*) / bianca → _____

2. maglietta (*t-shirt*) / rossa → _____

3. gonne (*skirt*) / corte → _____

4. giacca (*jacket*) / **molto*** economica _____

5. scarpe sportive (*sneakers*) / belle _____

*Molto: Is an adverb that means **very**. Adverbs go before adjectives and verbs. Check out some more adverbs here:

molto (*very*)	+ adjective/adverb	Quei fiori sono **molto** belli (*those flowers are very beautiful*)
tanto (*a lot*)	**+ verb**	Carlo viaggia **tanto** (*Carlos travels a lot*)
abbastanza (*quite*)	+ adjective/adverb/ verb	Lei cammina **abbastanza** veloce (*she walks quite fast*)
poco (*not a lot*)	+ adjective/adverb/ verb	Martino mangia **poco** (*Martín doesn't eat a lot*)
troppo (*too much*)	+ adjective/adverb/ verb	Elena parla **troppo** (*Elena talks too much*).

C. Complete these sentences with **questo, quello**.

1. Chi (*Who*) è _____ (that) dottore? (This)_____ dottore è un cardiologo (*cardiologist*).

2. _____ (This) pianeta è molto grande.

3. _____ (that over there) casa è bella.

4. _____ (that over there) treno è grande.

5. _____ (that) moto è nuova.

6. _____ (that) giovane è simpatico.

7. Lo studente è _____ (that over there) ragazzo laggiù.

D. The opposite. Complete each sentence with the correct form of **questo, questa, questi, queste**. Next answer in the reverse, using the adjective that means the opposite. **Example:** È buono _____ **professore?** _____: È buono questo **professore? No,** è cattivo.

1.   È felice ___ bambina? _____.

2.   Sono ricchi _____ ragazzi? _____

3.   È brutto ____ cane? _____

4.   Sono vecchi ____ edifici? _____

5.   È anziana ____ donna? _____

6.   Sono forti _____ ragazze? _____

7.   È grande ____ casa? _____

8.   È alto ____ bambino? _____

3 DESCRIBING PEOPLE AND ADJECTIVES IN THE PLURAL FORM

Remember when we talked about using è to describe a singular noun? Like, for example, **la donna è intelligente** to say, 'the woman is intelligent'?

It also becomes necessary to describe plural nouns in the same way. In English, 'is' becomes 'are' when we're talking about plural nouns, like in the sentence 'the books are boring.'

In Italian, è becomes **sono.**

Instead of...

lui è: *he* (*masculine*) *is*

lei è: *she* (*feminine*) *is*

You would say...

quelli sono: *they* (*masculine*) *are*

quelle sono: *they* (*feminine*) *are*

Just like è, you use the word **sono** regardless of whether the noun is feminine or masculine.

For example:

They (a group of men) are thin → Quelli **sono** magri.

They (a group of women) are intelligent → Quelle **sono** intelligenti.

Now, you know how to say 'he/she is' and 'they are'! Try and practice this with different adjectives.

Vocabulary: the neighbourhood

Time to expand your vocabulary! Let's look at some nouns that you'll encounter in your typical neighbourhood, town, and city.

Albero	[ahl-beh-roh]	*tree*
Fiore	[fyoh-reh]	*flower*
Strada	[strah-dah]	*street*
ufficio postale	[oof-fee-chee-oh poh-stah-leh]	*post office*
Pescheria	[peh-skeh-ree-ah]	*fish store*
Supermercato	[soo-pehr-mehr-kah-toh]	*supermarket*

Ufficio	[oof-fee-chee-oh]	*office*
Automobile	[aw-toh-moh-bee-leh]	*car*
Teatro	[teh-ah-troh]	*theatre*
Commesso	[kohm-mehs-soh]	*salesperson*
fruttivendolo	[froot-teeh-vehn-doh-loh]	*fruit and vegetable store*
Parco	[pahr-koh]	*park*
Giardino	[jahr-dee-noh]	*garden/yard*
Scuola	[skwoh-lah]	*school*
Università	[oo-nee-vehr-see-tah]	*college/university*
Cinema	[chee-neh-mah]	*movie theatre*
Chiesa	[kyeh-sah]	*church*
Aeroporto	[ah-eh-roh-pohr-toh]	*airport*
Museo	[moo-seh-oh]	*museum*
bar	[bahr]	*bar*
Ristorante	[reeh-stoh-rahn-teh]	*restaurant*
Viale	[vee-ah-leh]	*avenue*
edificio	[eh-dee-fee-chyoh]	*building*

3.1.   Practice

A. Imagine you're showing your friend around your block from your car. Point out some places of interest, completing the sentences with the right form of: **quello, quella, quelli, quelle**.

1.   _____ casa è molto grande. 2. _____ edificio (*building*) è l'ufficio postale (*post office*) e _____ albero è molto vecchio. 3. _____ strada (*street*) è nuova e _____ cani sono cattivi. 4. _____ viale è ampio.

B. Rewrite these sentences using the right form of the demonstrative adjective, of the verb *to be* (è or **sono**, depending on whether the subject is singular or plural), and the right form of the adjective (singular or plural).

Example: Questa / strada / è / lunga: Quest**e** strad**e sono** lungh**e**.

1.   Questo / sistema / è / eccellente _____

2.   Questa / pescheria / è / cara _____

3.   Questa / città / è / bella _____

4.   Questo / teatro / è / piccolo _____

5.   Quello / ufficio / è / nuovo _____

6.   Quella / automobile / è / gialla _____

Common Error: ────────────

Common Error: When using the word **persona**, avoid using a masculine adjective, even if the sex of the person you are referring to is male. **Persona** always agrees with a **feminine adjective**:

Giuseppe è una persona buono. X

Giuseppe è una **persona** buon**a**. ✓

Martino è una persona lavoratore. X

Martino è una **persona** lavoratr**ice**. ✓

Luigi è una persona simpatico. X

Luigi è una **persona** simpatic**a**. ✓

ANSWER KEY

Practice. 1.1

A. 1. fedele, intelligente, vecchia 2. nuovo, marrone 3. intelligente, lavoratrice, interessante, felice, fedele 4. veloce, nuovo, marrone 5. interessante, moro, veloce, felice, intelligente, fedele, alto, ricco 6. cara, vecchia, nuova, economica, marrone 7. nuovo, ricco, delizioso, marrone 8. lavoratrice, interessante, felice, intelligente, vecchia, fedele, anziana 9. cara, vecchia, nuova, economica 10. lavoratrice, interessante, felice, intelligente, vecchia, fedele, anziana 11. interessante, difficile, nuovo, facile 12. lavoratore, interessante, felice, intelligente 13. interessante, difficile, veloce, nuovo, facile 14. interessante, moro, veloce, felice, intelligente, fedele, alto, ricco 15. cara, interessante, vecchia, nuova 16. cara, vecchia, nuova, economica, marrone 17. interessante, difficile, facile 18. nuovo, ricco, delizioso

B.   1. gialla 2. blu 3. arancione 4. bianca 5. nera 6. grigio 7. verde 8. rosato 9. marrone 10. rosso

C.   1. Anche lui è gentile. 2. Anche questo è facile. 3. Anche loro sono lavoratori. 4. Anche loro sono grassi. 5. Anche lei è buona 6. Anche loro sono forti.

D.   1. alta, lavoratrice, bionda, felice e ricca. 2. grande, brutta, vecchia, cara e bassa. 3. povero, stupido, moro, basso, pigro e giovane.

Practice. 2.1

A.   1. Questa camicia è pulita 2. Queste scarpe sono care 3. Questo maglione è di lana 4. Questi vestiti sono di seta 5. Questi pantaloni sono economici.

B.   1. Quella casacca è bianca 2. Quella maglietta è rossa 3. Quelle gonne sono corte 4. Quella giacca è molto economica 5. Quelle scarpe sportive sono belle

C.   1. Chi è quel dottore? Quel dottore è un cardiologo. 2. Quel pianeta è molto grande. 3. Quella casa è bella. 4. Quel treno è lungo. 5. Quella moto è nuova. 6. Quel giovane è simpatico. 7. Lo studente è quel ragazzo laggiù.

D.   1. È felice questa bambina? No, è triste. 2. Sono ricchi questi ragazzi? No, sono poveri. 3. È brutto quel cane? No, è bello. 4. Sono vecchi questi edifici? No, sono nuovi. 5. È anziana questa donna? No, è giovane. 6. Sono forti queste ragazze? No, sono deboli. 7. È grande questa casa? No, è piccola. 8. È alto questo bambino? No, è basso.

Practice. 3.1

A.   1. Quella casa è molto grande. 2. Quell'edificio è l'ufficio postale e quell'albero è molto vecchio. 3. Quella strada è nuova e quei cani sono cattivi. 4. Quel viale è ampio.

B.   1. Questo sistema è eccellente. 2. Queste pescherie sono care. 3. Questa città è bella. 4. Questo teatro è piccolo. 5. Quegli uffici sono nuovi. 6. Quelle automobili sono gialle.

LESSON 05

TO BE OR NOT TO BE

THE VERB **ESSERE** (*TO BE*)

1 PRESENT TENSE OF ESSERE

Remember the words è and **sono**? They mean 'is' and 'are,' which are essentially the same thing, but one is singular and the other is plural. The Italian words è and **sono** are all rooted in the same Italian verb **essere**, which means 'to be.'

In English, we use the word è for basically everything. You use it to say both 'the car is red' (description) and 'the car is here' (location), even though you're describing different types of attributes about the car.

In Italian, you wouldn't use the same word for different types of descriptions.

Yes, you can say **l'automobile è rossa** (the car is red), but you can't use the same word to indicate the location of the car.

To indicate location, you would say **l'automobile <u>sta qui</u>** (the car is here).

Let's look at the two verbs in these sentences, è and **sta**. While è is rooted in the verb **essere**, which means 'to be,' **sta** is rooted in the verb **stare**. And guess what? It also means 'to be'! That's right, in English, **essere** and **stare** both mean the same thing, but in Italian, they describe different types of indications.

Before we learn more about **stare**, let's make sure you're familiar with all the forms of **essere**. You already know è and **sono** ('is' and 'are'), which can be used to say **lui/lei** è (he/she is) and **essi/esse sono** (they are). But what if you wanted to say, 'we are' or 'I am'? To refer to different pronouns, you'll need to make modifications.

Let's take a look at these modifications!

1.1.   Practice

Reading Comprehension

Read the following dialogue and use the table below (modifications for 'essere') to identify exactly what they're saying.

—— In città ——

TOMMASO: Scusi, questo è l'ufficio postale?

LUIGI: Mi dispiace, non **sono** di qui.

TOMMASO: Ah, di dov'**è** Lei?

LUIGI: **Sono** di un'altra città. Non **sono** di Roma.

TOMMASO: Ah, é un turista, come me.

LUIGI: Sí, **sono** un turista. **Sono** degli Stati Uniti. E Lei?

TOMMASO: **Sono** francese.

LUIGI: Ah. **Siamo** due turisti. Quella signora là è italiana. Lei è di qui.

Glossary:

Di qui: *from here*

Di dove...?: *Where... from?*

Un'altra: *another*

Come: *like*

Qui: *here*

---
essere *to be*

io (*I*)	**sono**	noi (*we*)	**siamo**
tu (*you*)	**sei**	voi (*you*)	**siete**
egli/lui (*he*)		essi (*they*)	
ella/lei (*she*)	è	esse (*they*)	**sono**
esso (*it*)		loro (*they*)	
Lei/Voi (*You – formal*)	**è/siete**		

We mentioned that verbs meaning 'to be' are used to describe things in different ways. So, when exactly is **essere** (io **sono, sei**, è, **sono,** etc) used? Generally, **essere** is used to describe:

- The nature of something or someone
- The identity of something or someone
- Time
- Events

This means you would use **essere** in these ten situations:

1. To *describe*

Io **sono** bionda = *I am blond*

> Tu **sei** alto = *You're tall*
>
> Lui è giovane = *He is young*
>
> Lei è intelligente = *She is intelligent*
>
> **Siamo** simpatici = *We are nice*
>
> Voi **siete** celibi = *You all are single*
>
> Voi **siete** romantici = *You all are romantic*
>
> Essi **sono** mori = *They are dark-haired*

TIP

Note that in Italian you do not need to add the pronoun to a sentence—unless you want to stress it—because it is already included in the verb: **siamo** simpatici (*we are nice*).

2. To *indicate a profession*

> Marco è avvocato = *Marcos is a lawyer*
>
> Io **sono** studente = *I am a student*
>
> Lei è architetta = *She is an architect*
>
> **Siamo** dottori = *We are doctors*

Siete professori = *You are professors*

Voi **siete** dirigenti = *You are managers*

Essi **sono** ingegneri = *They are engineers*

TIP

Unlike English, Italian omits the indefinite article **un/una** before an unmodified profession. For example: **Loro sono dottoresse**. But if you modify the profession, you need to add the indefinite article: **Loro sono delle dottoresse eccellenti.**

3. To *indicate where someone comes from*

Io **sono** del Perú = *I am from Peru*

Tu **sei** della Colombia = *You are from Colombia*

Lui è di New York = *He is from New York*

Lei è spagnola = *You are from Spain*

Noi **siamo** italiani = *We are from Italy*

Voi **siete** francesi = *You are all from France*

Essi **sono** irlandesi = *They are from Ireland*

4. To *identify specific attributes about a person, such as relationship, nationality, race, or religion*

Io **sono** cattolica = *I am Catholic*

Tu **sei** argentino = *You are Argentinian*

Lui è asiatico = *He is Asian*

Siamo celibi = *We are single*

Voi **siete** compagne di scuola = *You are student friends*

Marco e Luisa **sono** amici = *Marcos and Luisa are friends*

5.   To say *what material something is made of*

Il tavolo è di legno = *The table is of wood (The table is made of wood)*

La casa è di mattoni = *The house is of bricks (The house is made of bricks)*

La sedia è di plastica = *The chair is of plastic (The chair is made of plastic)*

Le scarpe **sono** di pelle = *The shoes are of leather (The shoes are made of leather)*

Le finestre **sono** di vetro = *The windows are of glass (The windows are made of glass)*

6.   To say *who something belongs to*

Il cane è di Maria = *The dog is of María (The dog belongs to Maria)*

Gli amici **sono** di Pietro = *The friends are of Pedro (The friends belong to Pedro).*

Il libro è del ragazzo = *The book is of the boy (The book belongs to the boy)*

La foto è di lei = *The photograph is of her (The photograph belongs to her)*

La moto è loro = *The motorcycle is of them (The motorcycle belongs to them).*

TIP

di + il = del. When **di** (*of*) is followed by **il** (*the*), the words contract to **del** (*of the*)

7.   To say for *whom or for what something is intended*

    Il televisore è per lei = *The television is for her*

    La matita è per loro = *The pencil is for them*

    La gatta è per mio fratello = *The female cat is for my brother*

8.   To describe *where an event takes place*

    La festa è a casa di Maria = *The party is in Maria's house*

    La cerimonia è all'università = *The ceremony is at the university*

9.   To *indicate a generalization*

    È importante studiare = *It's important to study*

10.   To express time, dates, and days of the week.

    Sono le 3:00 del pomeriggio = It's 3:00 p.m.

    È il 14 di agosto = It's August 14th

    È lunedì = It's Monday

TIP

Note that in Italian, the days of the week and the months of the year are NOT capitalized like in English.

Speak Abroad
Academy

Vocabulary: types of materials

carta	[kahr-tah]	*Paper*
legno	[leh-nyoh]	*Wood*
vetro	[ve-troh]	*Glass*
plastica	[plahs-tee-kah]	*Plastic*
metallo	[meh-tahl-loh]	*Metal*
tessuto	[tehs-soo-toh]	*Fabric*

1.2.   Practice

A. Answer these questions about the dialogue "La ciudad" at the beginning of the lesson:

1.   Di dov'è Luigi? _____

2.   Di dov'è Tommaso? _____

3.   In quale città stanno? _____

4.   Cosa sono Luigi e Tommaso? _____

5.   Di dov'è la signora?_____

B. Where are these famous people from? Use the 3rd person singular of **essere** *(to be)* to say where they are from and what nationality they are.

Inghilterra (*England*)   Francia (*France*)   Spagna (*Spain*)

Italia (*Italy*)   Portogallo (*Portugal*)   Messico (*Mexico*)

Stati Uniti (*the United States*)   Germania (*Germany*)

To be or not to be

Example: David Beckham: <u>È dell'Inghilterra. È inglese.</u>

1.   Luciano Pavarotti _____

2.   Frida Kahlo _____

3.   Johnny Depp _____

4.   Albert Einstein _____

5.   Coco Chanel _____

6.   Rafael Nadal _____

7.   Cristiano Ronaldo _____

8.   Paul McCartney _____

C. Complete the following sentences with the appropriate form of **essere** and include in parentheses *why* you're using this verb:

⊃   Description   ⊃   Possession

⊃   Profession   ⊃   For whom something is intended

⊃   Origin   ⊃   Generalizations

⊃   Identification   ⊃   Where an event takes place

⊃   Material something is made of   ⊃   Time, date, or day of the week

Example: Il ragazzo <u>è</u> simpatico. (description)

1.   Mick Jagger _____ inglese (_____)

2.   Le sedie _____ di plastica (_____)

3.   Noi _____ della Colombia (_____)

4.   I tavoli _____ di legno (_____)

5.   Il cibo _____ per la bambina (_____)

6.   _____ lunedì (_____)

7. Marco e Luigi _____ avvocati (_____)

8. La festa _____ nel club (_____)

9. Il cane _____ di Maria (_____)

10. Il libro _____ giallo (_____)

11. _____ il 14 di febbraio (_____).

D. What are these objects made of? Example: ¿De qué es la mesa? Es de madera.

1. Di cosa è fatta la bottiglia (*bottle*)? _____

2. Di cosa è fatta la sedia? _____

3. Di cosa è fatta la casa? _____

4. Di cosa sono fatte le scarpe? _____

5. Di cosa sono fatte le finestre? _____

6. DI cosa è fatto il pavimento (*floor*)? _____

7. Di cosa è fatta l'automobile? _____

8. Di cosa è fatta la pagina (*page*)? _____

E. Complete with the right form of the verb ser: è or **sono**, depending on the subject.

1. Il cane _____ di Maria.

2. Gli amici _____ di Marco.

3. La casa _____ di Teresa.

4. Le foto _____ dei nonni.

5. Le automobili _____ degli zii.

6. Il gatto _____ di Maria.

F. Now let's try to use all the forms of the verb "to be". Complete the sentences with the right form of the verb "to be" (**essere**) and the place suggested in each case. **Example: Io (Perú) Io sono del Perú**

1.   Essi (Germania) _____

2.   Tu e Alessandra (Argentina) _____

3.   Voi (Colombia) _____

4.   Noi (Messico) _____

5.   Io (Francia) _____

6.   Felipe (Brasil) _____

G. Use the right form of the verb **essere**:

1.   Voi _____ musulmani.

2.   Io _____ sposata.

3.   Noi _____ celibi.

4.   Martino _____ cinese.

5.   Elena e Sofia _____ brasiliane.

6.   Tu _____ bianco.

7.   Voi _____ cristiani.

8.   Maria _____ messicana.

9.   Tu e Martino _____ amici.

H. Translate the following sentences. Remember that you use **es** or **son** to express time, dates, and days of the week.

1.   It's three o'clock in the afternoon (tre del pomeriggio): _____

2.   It's first of May (primo di maggio): _____

3.   It's November 3rd (novembre): _____

4. It's Wednesday (mercoledì): _____

5. It's ten o'clock in the morning (dieci del mattino): _____

6. It's Sunday (domenica): _____

I. Answer these questions with the appropriate form of **essere**:

1. Lei è simpatico? _____

2. Siete studenti? _____

3. È piccola la casa di Marianna? _____

4. Di dov'è Elena? (Inghilterra) _____

5. Che cos'è importante? (studiare) _____

6. Che ore sono? (4:00 del pomeriggio) _____

J. Rewrite these sentences contracting di + il. **Example: L'automobile è del signor** Pérez: **L'automobile è del signor** Pérez.

1. I cani sono del bambino: _____

2. Il libro è del collegio: _____

3. Quella casa è del signore ricco: _____

4. La moto è del giovane: _____

5. Il cibo è del ristorante: _____

6. L'automobile è del ragazzo: _____

ANSWER KEY

Practice. 1.2

A.   1. Luigi è degli Stati Uniti. 2. Tomás è francese. 3. Stanno a Madrid. 4. Sono turisti. 5. La signora è di Madrid.

B.   1. Luciano Pavarotti è dell'Italia. È italiano. 2. Frida Kahlo è del Messico. È messicana. 3. Johnny Depp è degli Stati Uniti. È statunitense. 4. Albert Einstein è della Germania. È tedesco. 5. Coco Chanel è della Francia. È francese. 6. Rafael Nadal è della Spagna. È spagnolo. 7. Cristiano Ronaldo è del Portogallo. È portoghese. 8. Paul McCartney è dell'Inghilterra. È inglese.

C.   1. Mick Jagger è inglese (identification). 2. Le sedie sono di plastica (material something is made of). 3. Noi siamo della Colombia (origin). 4. I tavoli sono di legno (material something is made of). 5. Il cibo è per la bambina (for whom something is intended). 6. È lunedì (day of the week). 7. Marco e Luigi sono avvocati (profession). 8. La festa è nel club (where an event takes place). 9. Il cane è di Maria (possession). 10. Il libro è giallo (description). 11. È il 14 di febbraio (date).

D.   1. È di plastica o di vetro 2. È di legno o di plastica 3. È di mattoni 4. Sono di pelle 5. Sono di vetro 6. È di legno 7. È di metallo 8. È di carta

E.   1. è 2. sono 3. è 4. sono 5. sono 6. è

F.   1. Loro sono della Germania 2. Tu e Alejandra siete/siete dell'Argentina 3. Voi siete della Colombia 4. Noi siamo del Messico 5. Io sono della Francia. 6. Felipe è del Brasile.

G.   1. è 2. sono 3. siamo 4. è 5. sono 6. sei 7. siete 8. è 9. siete/siete

H.   1. sono le tre del pomeriggio 2. è il primo di maggio 3. è il 3 di novembre 4. è mercoledì 5. sono le dieci del mattino 6. è domenica

I.   1. Sì, sono simpatico 2. Sì, siamo studenti 3. No, non è piccola la casa di Marianna (or Sì, è piccola la casa di Marianna) 4. Elena è dell'Inghilterra 5. È importante studiare 6. Sono le 4:00 del pomeriggio

J.   1. I cani sono del bambino 2. Il libro è del collegio 3. Quella casa è del signore ricco 4. La moto è del giovane 5. Il cibo è del ristorante 6. L'automobile è del ragazzo

LESSON 06

I HAVE YOUR LOVE

STARE *(TO BE)* AND **AVERE** *(TO HAVE)*

1 PRESENT TENSE OF STARE *(TO BE)*

As we said in the previous chapter, **stare** also means 'to be.' However, it's used in different types of contexts and situations.

In Italian, **stare** is used to express:

- location: lei **sta** nella casa (*she is in the house*)

- health: lui **sta** male (*he is sick*)

- changing mood or condition: **stai** tranquillo (*be quiet*)

- personal opinion: Questo vestito ti **sta** bene (*You are fine with this dress*)

Notice that what most of these situations have is that they are changeable. He is sick, but he might not be sick soon. It's a temporary state, not a permanent one. 'Sick' is his condition, but it's not his nature.

When using **stare** for location, use the preposition **in + the article (il/lo, la/ i/ gli, le)**: **Sara sta nella casa.**

—————— **stare** *to be* ——————

io (*I*)	**sto**	noi (*we*)	**stiamo**
tu (*you*)	**stai**	voi (*you*)	**state**
egli/lui (*he*)		essi (*they*)	
ella/lei (*she*)	**sta**	esse (*they*)	**stanno**
esso (*it*)		loro (*they*)	

Lei/Voi (*You – formal*) **sta/state**

Vocabulary: more adjectives

Now let's learn some more adjectives to practice **stare**:

bello	[behl-loh]	*handsome*
magro	[mah-groh]	*thin*
stressato	[strehs-sah-toh]	*stressed*

stanco	[stahn-koh]	*tired*
contento	[kohn-tehn-toh]	*happy*
delizioso	[deh-lee-tsyoh-soh]	*delicious*
malato	[mah-lah-toh]	*sick*
arrabbiato	[ahr-rahb-byah-toh]	*angry*
delizioso	[deh-lee-tsyoh-soh]	*delicious*
pulito	[puh-lee-toh]	*clean*
sporco	[spohr-koh]	*dirty*
furioso	[foo-ryoh-soh]	*furious*
nervoso	[nehr-voh-soh]	*nervous*
occupato	[oh-koo-pah-toh]	*busy*
annoiato	[ahn-noh-yah-toh]	*bored*
preoccupato	[preh-ohk-koo-pah-toh]	*worried*
aperto	[ah-pehr-toh]	*open*
chiuso	[kyoo-soh]	*closed*

I have your love

1.1. Practice

A. Write the appropriate form of **stare**. Say why you chose that option:

➲ location   ➲ changing mood or condition

➲ health   ➲ personal opinion.

1. Parigi e Lione _____ in Francia. (_____)

2. La bambina _____ male. (_____)

3. _____ giù di morale. (_____)

4. Juan _____ a pezzi. (_____)

5. Noi _____ qui. (_____)

6. Il cibo _____ in frigorifero. (_____)

7. Voi _____ calmi. (_____)

8. Tu _____ dormendo. (_____)

B. And now, see if you can tell which verb to use, **essere** or **stare**, according to the meaning of each sentence, and match the verb to the subject in person and number.

Example: Maria e Juan <u>stanno</u> giù di morale.

1. Il tavolo e le sedie _____ in cucina.

2. Lui _____ avvocato.

3. Noi _____ stanchi.

4. _____ importante studiare.

5. Voi _____ all'università.

6. Martino e Luigi _____ intelligenti.

7. Il caffè _____ per la donna.

8. La città _____ bella.

9. Tu _____ una turista.

10. Io _____ del Guatemala.

11. La lezione _____ facile.

12. Il bambino _____ al collegio.

13. Voi _____ contenti.

14. Noi _____ italiani.

15. Sara _____ triste.

C. Make complete sentences using the appropriate form of **essere** or **stare** + the words between the parentheses.

Example: La nonna? (male) <u>La nonna sta male</u>

1. Tim? (spagnolo) _____

2. Il ristorante? (chiuso) _____

3. Le figlie di Pietro? (bionde e intelligenti) _____

4. Il problema? (molto facile) _____

5. Il libro? (interessante) _____

6. Tu? (furioso) _____

7. La banana? (gialla) _____

8. Noi? (felici) _____

9. La foto? (sedia) _____

I have your love

Common Mistake:

Of course, since English speakers only have one verb (*to be*) to express all these situations, it's completely normal to be confused about when to use each verb when speaking or writing in Italian. You'll get the hang of it with more practice!

Don't say: **Io sono bene**. X

The right way to say it is: **Io sto bene**. ✓ (changing mood).

D. Write **essere** or **stare** according to whether the adjective refers to an inherent feature or a changing condition. Example: **Lui ____ giù di morale → Lui sta giù di morale (changing condition).**

1. Lei _____ intelligente.

2. Egli _____ studioso.

3. Paula _____ furiosa.

4. Gli avvocati _____ occupati.

5. Il tavolo _____ sporco.

6. L'anziano _____ stanco.

7. L'anziano _____ simpatico.

8. La bambina _____ nervosa.

Summary of the Uses of Essere

➲	To describe	**Il fiore è bello**
➲	To indicate a profession	**Sono avvocatessa**
➲	To indicate someone's origin/nationality	**Loro sono del Messico**
➲	To identify inherent qualities about a person	**Lui è intelligente**
➲	To say what material something is made of	**La sedia è di plastica**
➲	To say who something belongs to	**Il libro è della bambina**

I have your love

⊃ To say for whom something is intended **Il cane è per lui**

⊃ To describe where an event takes place **La festa è nella casa**

⊃ To use a generalization È importante studiare

⊃ To express time, dates, and days of the week È martedì (*It's Tuesday*)

─── Summary uses of Stare ───

⊃ To express location **Sto nel ristorante**

⊃ To describe health **Maria sta male**

⊃ To express a changing mood or condition **Luigi sta giù di morale**

⊃ To express a personal opinion **Il vestito ti sta bene**

─── Common Mistake: ───

Keep in mind that **essere** is used to express **inherent** qualities of a person, such as...

Luisa è affettuosa. Luisa has a sweet-loving character. That's her nature. She is nice because that's who she is.

Stare is used to express a **transitory** condition, such as...

I have your love

> **Luisa sta a pezzi**. Luisa is tired now, but she won't be after she rests. ✓
>
> Don't say: **Luisa sta affettuosa**. X Say: **Luisa** è affettuosa.✓
>
> Don't say: **Luisa** è a pezzi. X Say: **Luisa sta a pezzi.**✓
>
> Don't say: **Io sono dormendo**. X Say: **Io sto dormendo.** ✓
>
> Don't say: **Mio padre è nel supermercato**. X Say: Mio padre sta nel supermercato.✓
>
> Don't say: **Lui sta medico**. X Say: **Lui è medico.** ✓

Then again, many adjectives can be used with either **essere** or **stare**, depending on the exact message that you're trying to convey. But as a rule, **essere** is used for unalterable qualities (**sono bionda**) and **stare** is used for variable qualities (**sto male**).

E. Say if these sentences are right (✓) or wrong (X) according to their use of essere or stare. **Example: Lui sta a pezzi X**

1.   Teresa e Miguel sono nel cinema _____

2.   Voi state male _____

3.   Questo vestito ti sta bene _____

4.   Tu sei un bravo studente _____

5.   Tu stai una brava avvocatessa _____

6.   Tu stai del Perú _____

7.   I fiori sono gialli _____

8.   Le sedie stanno di plastica _____

9.   Susanna sta intelligente _____

10. Miguel e Juan sono professori _____

11. La moto sta di Federico _____

12. Oggi sta mercoledì _____

F. Now take the ones that are wrong and rewrite them with the right verb:

_____

_____

_____

_____

2 PRESENT TENSE OF AVERE (*TO HAVE*)

Now that we're getting the hang of different verbs. Let's introduce another one! **Avere** is an extremely useful verb to know as it indicates that you possess something. In English this would mean 'to have.'

---
avere *to have*
---

io (*I*)	**ho**	noi (*we*)	**abbiamo**
tu (*you*)	**hai**	voi (*you*)	**avete**
egli/lui (*he*)		essi (*they*)	
ella/lei (*she*)	**ha**	esse (*they*)	**hanno**
esso (*it*)		loro (*they*)	

Lei/Voi (*You – formal*) **ha/avete**

I have your love

Listen to a Song

How do you feel about listening to a song while practicing the verb **avere**? This song belongs to David Rodrígez Labault, a Latin Grammy-winning Puerto Rican singer, whose stage name is Siete (Seven). https://youtu.be/Cij71bcdr1l

These are the lyrics to his song. Try listening to it first, reading the words, and after you understand it, try singing it while you listen to it again. We know there are a lot of new words, but don't worry. This will help you train your ear and start to recognize new sounds.

Non **ho** un cellulare tempestato di diamanti	*I don't have a diamond-studded cell*
Di tanti carati per poter fare colpo	*full of carats to impress others*
Ma **ho** una buona conversazione	*But I have good conversation*
Con cui ti faccio innamorare sempre più	*to make you fall more in love with me.*
Non **ho** un jet privato	*I don't have a private jet*
Comprato con la Black Card	*that I bought with the Black Card*
Ma **ho** un vecchio furgone	*but I have an old van*
Con cui andiamo sempre in giro	*that we always go on a ride on.*
Non **ho** roba di Versace	*I don't have Versace clothes*
Né muscoli sodi da mostrare	*nor hard muscles to show off*
Ma **ho** un paio di braccia nude	*but I have a pair of bare arms*
Che ti abbracceranno forte	*that will embrace you really tight.*

Non sono come Mariah Carey	*I'm not like Mariah Carey*
Con una jacuzzi piena di acqua Evian	*with a jacuzzi full of Evian water.*
Ma **ho** una capanna sulla spiaggia	*But I have a little hut on the beach,*
Per farti bagnare con l'acqua di mare	*so you can bathe in sea water.*
Ricky **ha** una bella faccia	*Ricky has a cute face,*
Enrique Iglesias i milioni	*Enrique Iglesias, the millions,*
e Aventura le villone	*And Aventura, the mansions,*
Ma...	*But*
Io **ho** il tuo amore	*I have your love*
Ho il tuo amore	*I got your love*
Io **ho** il tuo amore	*I have your love*
Io **ho** il tuo amore, yeah	*I have your love, yeah*
Io **ho** il tuo amore	*I have your love*
Io ho il tuo amore	*I got your love*
Io **ho** il tuo amore	*I have your love*
Io **ho** il tuo amore, yeah	*I have your love, yeah*

Tanto and Poco

You can also describe nouns by saying something about their quantity. In English, we might say something like 'many dogs' or 'a few dogs.' There are words for these descriptors in Italian, too. Unlike regular adjectives, they go *before* the noun instead of after.

Tanto/a/i/e (*a lot, many*)

This word must agree in gender and plurality with the noun they're in front of. E.g. **Ho tanti cani** (I have many dogs).

Tanto can also be an adverb, and remains invariable. Adverbs are words that describe verbs: **legge tanto** (*he reads a lot*).

Poco/a/chi/che (*little, few, not many*)

This word also must agree in gender and plurality with the noun, too! E.g. **Ho pochi vestiti** (*I have few dresses*).

Poco can also be an adverb, which means that it describes a verb, not just a noun. E.g. **Martino mangia poco** (*Martín doesn't eat much*).

2.1. Practice

A. Complete the sentences with the correct form of **avere**. Example: **Voi _____ tanti ospiti → Voi <u>avete</u> tanti ospiti.**

1. Noi _____ una casa molto bella.

2. Sofia e Paolo _____ sei televisioni.

3. Tu e Sara _____ tanti libri.

4. La nonna _____ pochi problemi.

5. Io _____ due mani.

6. Il cinema _____ tanti posti a sedere.

7. Quel giardino _____ tanti alberi.

8. Roberto e io _____ un ristorante.

9. Tu _____ un giardino molto bello.

10. Quel museo _____ tanti quadri interessanti.

Avere to Express Age

In Italian, we use the verb **avere** (*to have*) to say how old we are. Instead of saying you *are of* a certain age, you say that you *have* a certain number of years.

I am [number] years old = Ho [number] anni.

In Italian, you cannot omit the word **anni** in this expression.

As for numbers, we'll dive into them more extensively in the next chapter! But for now, here are some translations of sentences expressing age.

I have your love

Ho trent'anni	*I am thirty years old*
Hai ventitré anni	*You are twenty-three years old*
Lui/lei ha quarant'anni	*He/she is forty years old*
Abbiamo quindici anni	*We are fifteen years old*
Avete tutti due anni	*You all are two years old*
Hanno diciotto anni	*They are eighteen years old*

─────── Common Mistake: ───────

Of course, English speakers tend to translate the structure they use in English directly into Italian. This doesn't always work! In Italian, you never use the verbs **essere** (*to be*) or **stare** (*to be*) to talk about age. You use the verb **avere**.

Don't say: **Io sono vent'anni**. X

Don't say: **Io sto vent'anni.** X

The right way to say it is: **Io ho vent'anni**. ✓

2.2. Practice

Write the correct form of **avere** to convey these people's ages:

1. Manuel e José _____ ventuno anni.

2. Io _____ cinquant'anni.

3. Tu _____ diciotto anni.

4. Marina e io _____ trent'anni.

5. Voi _____ venticinque anni.

6. Mio nonno _____ settant'anni.

7. Mia nonna _____ sessantacinque anni.

8. Esse _____ quarantadue anni.

B. Indicate if these sentences are right (✓) or wrong (X). Remember, to express age in Italian you use the verb **avere**, not **essere** or **stare** like in English. **Example: Lui sta vent'anni. X Lui ha vent'anni.** ✓

1. Noi siamo sessant'anni. _____

2. Voi state quarant'anni. _____

3. Io ho cinquantadue anni. _____

4. José e Daniele hanno trentacinque anni. _____

5. Tu sei quindici anni. _____

6. Maria sta sei anni. _____

7. Tu e Miguel siete settanta anni. _____

8. Josefina sta ventitré anni. _____

I have your love

C. Now take the ones that were wrong and rewrite them with the correct verb:

_____

_____

_____

_____

D. Complete the following sentences using the correct verb form of **avere**.

1.   Io _____ tante scarpe.

2.   Noi _____ tanti amici.

3.   Marco _____ un libro.

4.   Tu _____ tanti gatti.

5.   Voi _____ una nonna buona.

6.   Lei _____ una matita rossa.

7.   Carlo e Maria _____ una figlia.

8.   Voi _____ un sistema eccellente.

9.   Laura _____ 32 anni.

ANSWER KEY

Practice. 1.1

A.   1. Parigi e Lione stanno in Francia (location). 2. La bambina sta male (health). 3. Sta giù di morale (changing mood). 4. Juan sta a pezzi (changing condition). 5. Noi stiamo qui (location). 6. Questo vestito ti sta bene (personal opinion). 7. Voi state meglio (changing mood). 8. Tu stai a pezzi (changing condition).

B.   1. Il tavolo e le sedie sono sporchi. 2. Lui è avvocato. 3. Noi stiamo a pezzi. 4. È importante studiare. 5. Voi state nell'università. 6. Martino e Luigi sono intelligenti. 7. Il caffè è per la donna. 8. La città è bella. 9. Tu sei una turista. 10. Io sono del Guatemala. 11. La lezione è facile. 12. Il bambino sta nel collegio. 13. Voi state bene. 14. Noi siamo italiani. 15. Sara sta giù di morale.

C.   1. Tim è spagnolo. 2. Il ristorante è chiuso. 3. Le figlie di Pietro sono bionde e intelligenti. 4. Il problema è molto facile. 5. Il libro è interessante. 6. Tu stai bollendo di rabbia. 7. La banana è gialla. 8. Noi stiamo esultando. 9. La foto sta sulla sedia.

D.   1. è 2. è 3. sta 4. stanno 5. sta 6. sta 7. è 8. sta

E.   1. X 2. X 3. X 4. ✓ 5. X 6. X 7. ✓ 8. X 9. X 10. ✓ 11. X 12. X

F.   1. Teresa e Miguel stanno nel cinema 2. Voi state male 3. L'università è buona 5. Tu sei una brava avvocatessa 6. Io sono del Perú 8. Le sedie sono di plastica 9. Susanna è intelligente 11. La moto è di Federico 12. Oggi è mercoledì

Practice. 2.1

A.   1. abbiamo 2. hanno 3. avete/avete 4. ha 5. ho 6. ha 7. ha 8. abbiamo 9. hai 10. ha

Practice. 2.2

B.   1. hanno 2. Ho 3. hai 4. abbiamo 5. avete 6. ha 7. ha 8. hanno

C.   1. X 2. X 3. ✓ 4. ✓ 5. X 6. X 7. X 8. X

D.   1. Noi abbiamo sessant'anni. 2. Voi avete quarant'anni. 5. Tu hai quindici anni. 6. Maria ha sei anni. 7. Tu e Miguel avete/avete settant'anni. 8. Josefina ha ventitré anni.

E.   1. ho 2. abbiamo 3. ha 4. hai 5. avete 6. ha 7. hanno 8. ha 9. ha

I have your love

ONE, TWO, BUCKLE MY SHOE

NUMBERS

If we're going to express the quantity of something, we obviously need to know our numbers. Just like in English, they're also essential for telling the date and time!

1 NUMBERS

0 zero	[tseh-roh]	*zero*
1 uno	[oo-noh]	*one*
2 due	[doo-eh]	*two*
3 tre	[treh]	*three*

4	quattro	[kwaht-troh]	four
5	cinque	[cheen-kweh]	five
6	sei	[say]	six
7	sette	[seht-teh]	seven
8	otto	[oht-toh]	eight
9	nove	[noh-veh]	nine
10	dieci	[dee-eh-chee]	ten
11	undici	[oon-dee-chee]	eleven
12	dodici	[doh-dee-chee]	twelve
13	tredici	[treh-dee-chee]	thirteen
14	quattordici	[kwaht-tohr-dee-chee]	fourteen
15	quindici	[kween-dee-chee]	fifteen
16	sedici	[seh-dee-chee]	sixteen
17	diciassette	[dee-chee-ahs-seht-teh]	seventeen
18	diciotto	[dee-chee-oht-toh]	eighteen
19	diciannove	[dee-chee-ahn-noh-veh]	nineteen
20	venti	[vehn-teeh]	twenty

One, two, buckle my shoe

─────── The number one in Italian: ───────

Uno is the form you used when counting: **Uno, due tre...**

Un is the form you use before masculine singular nouns: **un cane**

Una is the form you use before feminine singular nouns: **una casa**

1.1.   Practice

A. Complete with **Uno, Una,** or **Un** according to each sentence. **Example: ___ cane → <u>Un</u> cane.**

1.   Ha _____ anno.

2.   Ha _____ matita.

3.   Abbiamo _____ gatta.

4.   _____, due, tre, quattro.

5.   _____ uomo sta camminando (*a man is walking*).

6.   _____ fiore giallo

2 THERE IS AND THERE ARE: *C'È*

Statements with c'è

The word **c'è** (pronounced like the English *cheh*) means 'there is' and 'there are.' As you know, it's a useful way of describing the contents or arrangement of something. You can also use **c'è** to turn something into a sentence by essentially saying 'is there?' or 'are there?'

You'll be relieved to know that **c'è** is used for both singular and plural nouns. Whether you're talking about one cat in the house or more than one cat in the house, you would still use **c'è** in either case.

C'è un gatto in casa (singular)

Ci sono gatti in casa (plural)

────── Common Mistake: ──────

Don't use the Italian definite articles **il/lo, la, i/gli,** and **le** (*the*) after **c'è**. Use, instead, the definite articles after **c'è**: **un, dei, una, delle.**

Don't say: **C'è la matita sul tavolo.** X

Say: **C'è una matita sul tavolo** (*there is a pencil on the table*) ✓

One, two, buckle my shoe

TIP

When **c'è** is followed by a plural noun, you don't need the article:

Don't say: **Ci sono i fiori nel giardino**. X

Say: **Ci sono fiori nel giardino**. ✓

Ci sono quindici cani per strada	*There are fifteen dogs in the street*
C'è una persona nell'ufficio	*There is one person in the office*
C'è un albero nel cortile	*There is a tree in the yard*
C'è tanto cibo nel supermercato	*There is a lot of food in the supermarket*
Ci sono due turiste tedesche sul treno	*There are two German tourists on the train*

2.1. Practice

A. Look at these sentences and decide if you should leave them as they are (write a checkmark next to them) or if they need to be changed. In that case, write the correct sentence next to them.

Example: **C'è un gatto nel giardino** ✓

1.   C'è il tappeto nella casa. _____

2.   Ci sono le tigri allo zoo. _____

3.   Ci sono mele dal fruttivendolo. _____

4.   C'è un quadro nel museo. _____

5. Ci sono gli uffici nell'edificio. _____

6. Ci sono tanti bambini nel collegio. _____

7. Ci sono i turista in città. _____

8. Ci sono le persone nel cinema. _____

The Negative with C'è

To make a sentence negative, just add a **non** before **c'è**:

Non ci sono quindici cani per strada.   *There are not fifteen dogs in the street.*

Non ci sono due turiste tedesche sul treno. *There are not two German tourists on the train.*

The Interrogative With C'è

To ask a question with **c'è**, follow the same order as with the statement, but just add a question mark at the end of the sentence. If you're speaking this sentence out loud, you can use the tone of your voice to indicate that you're asking a question, just like you do in English. With a simple rising intonation, you can convey that you're asking a question, not making a statement.

Ci sono due cani per strada?	*Are there two dogs in the street?*
C'è una persona in ufficio?	*Is there one person in the office?*
C'è un albero nel giardino?	*Is there a tree in the yard?*

One, two, buckle my shoe

C'è tanti cibo nel supermercato?	*Is there a lot of food in the supermarket?*
Ci sono due turiste tedesche sul treno?	*Are there two German tourists on the train?*

Difference between c'è and stare

Use **c'è** (there is/there are) when you're talking about the existence of something/ someone. For example, **c'è un museo nella mia città** (*There is a museum in my city*).

Use **stare,** which means 'to be,' when you're talking about where something or someone *is*. For example, **il collegio sta dietro l'angolo** (*The school is on the corner*)

2.2. Practice

A. Translate the following to English:

Example: Ci sono matite in casa tua? <u>Ci sono matite in casa tua?</u>

1. Ci sono fiori nel giardino? _____

2. Ci sono sedie nell'ufficio? _____

3. Ci sono gatti per strada? _____

4. Ci sono hotel in città? _____

5. C'è un televisore in casa? _____

6. Ci sono dottori all'ospedale? _____

7. C'è un cane nell'automobile? _____

8. C'è una radio nell'automobile? _____

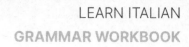
9. Ci sono due donne nella pescheria?_____

10. Ci sono tavoli nel ristorante? _____

B. Turn these affirmative sentences into negative sentences. Place **no** before **c'è**.

1. Ci sono animali allo zoo: _____

2. Ci sono tanti bambini al parco: _____

3. C'è un telefono pubblico in strada: _____

4. C'è tanta gente al ristorante: _____

5. C'è un buon hotel in città: _____

6. Ci sono tanti pianeti nel cielo: _____

C. Fill in the blanks with **c'è** or **sta**:

1. Dove _____ l'ufficio postale?

2. Nel collegio _____ un grande parco.

3. La chiesa _____ è dietro l'angolo.

4. L'università _____ accanto al parco.

5. _____ ristoranti molto buoni nella mia città.

6. Sulla piazza centrale _____ due bar.

7. _____ un parco lì?

8. Sí, il parco _____ lì.

9. Dove _____ il parco?

10. _____ un parco vicino.

3   *TO DO/TO MAKE*: FARE

Let's learn some more verbs. **Fare** is a useful verb that allows you to say, 'to do' or 'to make.' It's helpful when we're talking about activities!

Fare is an irregular verb like some of the others we've covered, which means that it looks different depending on the pronouns that are next to it.

---

fare *to do/to make*

io (*I*)	**faccio**	noi (*we*)	**facciamo**
tu (*you*)	**fai**	voi (*you*)	**fate**
egli/lui (*he*)		essi (*they*)	
ella/lei (*she*)	**fa**	esse (*they*)	**fanno**
esso (*it*)		loro (*they*)	

Lei/Voi (*You – formal*) **fa/fate**

Fare is an irregular verb of the 1st conjugation (suffix *-are*). It can also be used to talk about the weather in an impersonal way. In this case, we use it as a third-person verb, just like we would use it for the pronouns for 'he' or 'she.' It looks like this...

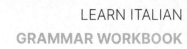

It's cold: **fa freddo**

It's hot: **fa caldo**

It's funny: **fa ridere**

It's sad: **fa piangere**

Vocabulary: the weather

Nuvole: clouds → ci sono nuvole/si sta annuvolando

Pioggia: rain → c'è pioggia/sta piovendo/piove

Neve: snow → c'è neve/sta nevicando/nevica

Vento: wind → c'è vento/sta soffiando il vento

3.1.   Practice

A. Say what the weather is like according to what people are wearing/doing:

1.   Maria is wearing shorts and a T-shirt: _____

2.   Tommaso is wearing a scarf, gloves, and a jacket: _____

3.   Luigi is wearing a windbreaker: _____

4.   Teresa is wearing sunblock: _____

5.   Paola is wearing a raincoat: _____

6.   Guillermo is looking at the snow through the window: _____

7.   Carlo is looking at the clouds in the sky: _____

One, two, buckle my shoe

Vocabulary: everyday objects

la valigia	[lah vah-lee-jah]	*the suitcase*
l'esercizio	[leh-sehr-chee-tsyoh]	*the exercise*
il compito	[eel kohm-pee-toh]	*the homework*
lo yoga	[loh yoh-gah]	*the yoga*
lo sport	[loh spohrt]	*the sports*
il nuoto	[eel nwoh-toh]	*the swimming*
la colazione	[lah koh-lah-tsyoh-neh]	*the breakfast*
il pranzo	[eel prahn-tsoh]	*the lunch*
il tè	[eel teh]	*the teatime*
la cena	[lah cheh-nah]	*the dinner*

B. Use the appropriate form of **fare** (*to do/to make*) in these sentences:

1.   Noi _____ le valigie (*suitcases*).

2.   Juan e Isabella _____ un dolce.

3.   Io _____ esercizio (*exercise*)

4.   I bambini _____ il compito (*homework*)

5.   _____ caldo.

6.   Mia sorella _____ yoga.

7.   Tu _____ sport.

One, two, buckle my shoe

8. Voi _____ nuoto.

9. _____ tanto freddo.

4 THE INTERROGATIVE QUANTO/A? QUANTI/E?

Questions are important! How else can we discover information from other people? Let's start off with some of the most important interrogative words for everyday life.

Quanto/a?   *How much?*

Quanti/e?   *How many?*

In English, 'much' is used for nouns that are uncountable, whereas 'many' is for nouns that are countable. It's the same in Italian!

When you're asking someone how much coffee they want, you're expecting a reply like 'a lot' or 'not that much,' which is uncountable. However, if you were to phrase it as how *many* coffees they want, you're expecting a countable response like 'two cups' or 'just one.'

Keep this same rule in mind when determining whether to use **quanto/a** (not countable) or **quanti/e** (countable).

4.1. Practice

A. Fill in the blanks with the right form of quanto/a or quanti/e.

1. _____ cani avete?

2. _____ cibo c'è al supermercato?

3. _____ gatti ci sono nel parco?

4. _____ fiori ci sono nel giardino?

5. _____ lingue parli (*speak*)?   6. _____ caffè c'è?

B. Now we're going to tie in **quanti?** with **c'è**. Answer the following questions using the written number.

Example: **Quanti** sofà **ci sono** in casa tua? **Ci sono** due sofà in casa mia.

1. Quanti giorni ci sono in una settimana (*week*)? _____

2. Quante settimane (*weeks*) ci sono in un mese (*month*)? _____

3. Quanti mesi ci sono in un anno (*year*)? _____

4. Quanti giorni ci sono in un fine settimana (*weekend*)? _____

5. Quanti giorni ci sono nel mese di febbraio (February)? _____

6. Quante dita (*fingers*) ci sono nella tua (*your*) mano? _____

7. Quanti ospedali ci sono nella tua (*your*) città? _____

8. Quanti televisori hai nella tua (*your*) casa? _____

9. Quanti alberi ci sono nel tuo (*your*) giardino? _____

10. Quante sedie ci sono in casa tua? _____

C. Write sentences with the words that are suggested. Modify the words as needed to match the nouns and numbers and add articles when necessary. **Example: Ci sono/ tre/ elefante/allo/zoo: Ci sono tre elefanti allo zoo.**

1. ci sono/due/università/in/città _____

2. ci sono/venti/mele/nel/cestino (*basket*) _____

3. ci sono/dodici/mese/in/anno _____

4. c'è/una/Statua della Libertà/a/New York _____

5. ci sono/due/occhi/sul/viso _____

6. ci sono/tanto/edificio/in/città _____

ANSWER KEY

Practice. 1.1

A.	1. un 2. un 3. una 4. uno 5. un 6. una

Practice. 2.2

B.	1. X C'è un tappeto nella casa. 2. X Ci sono tigri allo zoo. 3. ✓ 4. ✓ 5. X Ci sono uffici nell'edificio. 6. ✓ 7. X Ci sono turista in città. 8. X Ci sono persone nel cinema.

Practice. 2.3

A.	1. Ci sono fiori nel giardino? 2. Ci sono sedie nell'ufficio? 3. Ci sono gatti per strada? 4. Ci sono hotel in città? 5. C'è un televisore nella casa? 6. Ci sono dottori nell'ospedale? 7. C'è un cane nell'auto? 8. C'è una radio nell'auto? 9. Ci sono due donne nella pescheria? 10. Ci sono tavoli in un ristorante?

B.	1. Non ci sono animali nello zoo. 2. Non ci sono tanti bambini al parco. 3. Non c'è un telefono pubblico per strada. 4. Non c'è tanta gente nel ristorante. 5. Non c'è un buon hotel in città. 5. Non ci sono tanti pianeti in cielo.

C.	1. sta 2. C'è 3. sta 4. sta 5. C'è 6. C'è 7. C'è 8. C'è 9. sta 10. C'è

Practice. 3.1

A.	1. fa caldo 2. fa freddo 3. c'è vento/sta soffiando il vento 4. c'è il sole 5. Sta piovendo/c'è pioggia/piove 6. c'è neve/sta nevicando/nevica 7. si sta annuvolando/ci sono nuvole

B.	1. facciamo 2. fanno 3. faccio 4. fanno 5. fa 6. fa. 7. fai 8. fate 9. fa

Practice. 4.1

A.   1. quanti 2. quanta 3. quanti 4. quante 5. quanti 6. quanto

B.   1. Ci sono sette giorni in una settimana. 2. Ci sono quattro settimane in un mese. 3. Ci sono 365 giorni in un anno. 4. Ci sono due giorni in un fine settimana. 5. Ci sono ventotto giorni nel mese di febbraio. 6. Ci sono cinque dita nella mia mano. 7. Ci sono due (number varies) ospedali nella mia città. 8. Ci sono diversi (number varies) televisori in casa mia. 9. Ci sono tre (number varies) alberi nel mio giardino. 10. Ci sono venti (number varies) sedie nella mia casa.

C.   1. Ci sono due università in città. 2. Ci sono venti mele nel cestino. 3. Ci sono dodici mesi in un anno. 4. C'è una Statua della Libertà a New York. 5. Ci sono due occhi sul viso. 6. Ci sono tanti edifici in città.

LESSON 08

TO KNOW IS KNOWING YOU KNOW NOTHING

SAPERE AND CONOSCERE

1 | TO KNOW: SAPERE

The verb **sapere** means 'to know' in English. However, just like some of the verbs we've discussed in prior chapters, it's not the only Italian verb that has this meaning! **Sapere** refers to a very specific type of knowledge. It's only used when we're talking about knowing facts, information, and skills. It *can't* be used when talking about knowing people, places, or things.

When *know* refers to *knowing facts* and *learned skills*, use **sapere**.

For example, **so la matematica** (*I know mathematics*) or **so nuotare** (*I know how to swim*).

---

sapere *to know facts*

io (*I*)	**so**	oi (*we*)	**sappiamo**
tu (*you*)	**sai**	voi (*you*)	**sapete**
egli/lui (*he*)		essi (*they*)	
ella/lei (*she*)	**sa**	esse (*they*)	**sanno**
esso (*it*)		loro (*they*)	

Lei/Voi (*You – formal*) **sa/sapete**

Sapere is an irregular verb and belongs to the 2nd conjugation (suffix *-ere*). But the irregularity is in its conjugation. For example, io **so**, which is used when talking about yourself in singular form. Normally, with regular verbs that end in *-ere*, you would knock off the *ere*, and add an *o* (**sapo** X). But with **sapere**, it's just **so** if you're talking only about yourself.

For example:

Io so (I know). **Non so** (I don't know).

1.1. Practice

A. Write the appropriate form of the verb **saber** in each sentence.

1. Noi _____ l'italiano.

2. Tu _____ il telefono di Luigi.

3. Voi _____ la verità.

4. Elena _____ quel poema?

5. Io _____ il francese (*French*).

6. Maria _____ la lezione.

7. Pietro e José _____ il tedesco (*German*)

8. Lui _____ ballare il valzer (*dance the waltz*)

2 TO KNOW: *CONOSCERE*

The other word for 'to know' is **conoscere.** Unlike **sapere,** you would use **conoscere** when talking about knowing certain people or things.

When *know* refers to *being familiar or being acquainted with something or someone,* use **conoscere**. For example, **conosco Luigi** (*I know Luis*).

To know is knowing you know nothing

---

conoscere *to be familiar with or to meet*

io (*I*)   **conosco**   noi (*we*) **conosciamo**

tu (*you*)   **conosci**   voi (*you*) **conoscete**

egli/lui (*he*)   essi (*they*)

ella/lei (*she*) **conosce** esse (*they*) **conoscono**

esso (*it*)   loro (*they*)

Lei/Voi (*You – formal*) **conosce/conoscete**

Conoscere is also an irregular verb of the 2nd conjugation (suffix *-ere*).

For example:

Io conosco (*I know*). **Non conosco** (*I don't know*).

2.1. Practice

A. Write the appropriate form of the verb **conoscere** in each sentence.

1.   Elena e Pietro _____ la professoressa

2.   Juan _____ il dottor Pérez.

3.   Voi _____ il sistema.

4. Noi _____ il cibo francese.

5. Io _____ la casa.

6. Maria _____ la città.

7. Tu _____ il Louvre.

8. Lui _____ il turista.

B. Now let's see if you can tell when to use sapere and when to use conoscere. Choose one of the two and conjugate it to make it fit in the sentence: Example: Maria _____ (conoscere/sapere) l'inglese → Maria sa l'inglese.

1. Tommaso _____ (conoscere/sapere) il sud della Spagna.

2. Voi _____ (conoscere/sapere) contare fino a dieci in tedesco.

3. Elena e Paolo _____ (conoscere/sapere) giocare a golf.

4. Non _____ (lui/conoscere/sapere) se fa freddo.

5. Maria _____ (conoscere/sapere) quel viale.

6. Tu _____ (conoscere/sapere) quella storia.

7. Io _____ (conoscere/sapere) dove vive Jorge (*where Jorge lives*).

8. Tu e Sara _____ (conoscere/sapere) le regole del Monopoli.

C. Here, you are required to choose the right verb and conjugate it. You do not need to use the pronoun; it's just a cue to tell you how to conjugate the verb.

1. _____ (io/conoscere/sapere) Mattia.

2. Non _____ (noi/conoscere/sapere) dove sta il gatto.

3. _____ (voi/conoscere/sapere) molto bene le opere di Albéniz.

4. Mia sorella non _____ (conoscere/sa) quel gruppo musicale (*band*).

5. _____ (tu/sapere/conoscere) a che ora inizia (*starts*) il film?

6. I miei cugini _____ (sapere/conoscere) cinque lingue.

To know is knowing you know nothing

7. _____ (io/conoscere/sapere) il Brasile molto bene.

8. _____ (lui/conoscere/sapere) il tuo fidanzato (*boyfriend*)?

9. Isabella e Luisa _____ (conoscere/sapere) la lezione molto bene.

3 SAPERE + INFINITIVE: TO KNOW HOW TO DO SOMETHING

We've mentioned a lot of infinitive verbs so far. In fact, **sapere** itself is an infinitive verb. It's the root word of every word, which means "to know "or "to play." When you use **sapere** before an infinitive verb, you're saying that you *know* how to do something.

So parlare francese (*I know how to speak French*).

Here are some verbs and specific activities in the infinitive form that you can combine with **sapere** to express your knowledge of a certain ability. Like, for example, **sa nuotare** (*he knows how to swim*), **sa parlare spagnolo** (*he knows how to speak Spanish*).

Which of the following do you know how to do?

nuotare	[nwoh-tah-reh]	*to swim*
ballare	[bahl-lah-reh]	*to dance*
cantare	[kahn-tah-reh]	*to sing*
fare ginnastica artistica	[fah-reh jeen-nah-stee-kah ahr-tee-stee-kah]	*to do artistic gymnastics*
giocare a tennis	[joh-kah-reh ah then-nees]	*to play tennis*

To know is knowing you know nothing

suonare il pianoforte	[swoh-nah-reh eel pyah-noh-fohr-teh]	*to play the piano*
giocare a pallacanestro	[joh-kah-reh ah pahl-lah-kah-neh-stroh]	*to play basketball*
giocare a golf	[joh-kah-reh ah golf]	*to play golf*
giocare a calcio	[joh-kah-reh a kahl-chee-oh]	*to play football*
scrivere romanzi	[skree-veh-reh roh-mahn-tsee]	*to write novels*
parlare	[pahr-lah-reh]	*to speak*
recitare	[reh-chee-tah-reh]	*to act*

3.1. Practice

A. What do these people know how to do? Use the verb saber + the right infinitive and direct object to complete the sentences. Example: **Serena Williams sa giocare a tennis.**

1.   Novak Djokovic _____

2.   LeBron James _____

3.   Tiger Woods _____

4.   J. K. Rowling _____

5.   Lionel Messi e Cristiano Ronaldo _____

6.   Taylor Swift _____

7.   Michael Phelps _____

8.   Shakira _____

9.   Meryl Streep _____

10.   Simon Biles _____

To know is knowing you know nothing

B. Who do these famous people know? Write the appropriate sentence, picking a person from the right row and finding the correct match on the left.

Sherlock Holmes	Dakota Johnson
Ashton Kutcher	Eva
Rhett Butler	Hailey Bieber
Chris Martin	Victoria Beckham
David Beckham	Watson
Adán	Scarlett O'Hara
Justin Bieber	Mila Kunis

1. _____

2. _____

3. _____

4. _____

5. _____

6. _____

7. _____

C. Write a sentence following the cues given:

Example: (conoscere)_____. (Laura/la zia Julia) → Laura conosce la zia Julia

1. (conoscere) _____ (io/il professor Blanco)

2. (conoscere) _____ (mia sorella e io/la madre di Juan)

3. (conoscere) _____ (Maria e Luigi/Sergio)

4. (conoscere) _____ (voi/direttore dell'area commerciale)

5. (conoscere) _____ (tu/zia Julia)

6. (conoscere) _____ (Carlos/la zia Julia)

7. (conoscere) _____ (Martino e Elena/la zia Julia)

D. Translate using **sapere** or **conoscere** depending on the context. Remember:

Conoscere = to be familiar with something or someone.

Sapere = to know facts and learned skills.

1. I know the truth _____

2. She knows Maria _____

3. They know how to swim _____

4. Pedro and Elena know New York _____

5. We know the answer _____

6. We know the student _____

7. You know my name _____

8. He knows the truth _____

9. The dog knows Juan _____

10. I know how to play the piano _____

11. We know the university _____

E. **Sapere or Conoscere? Choose the right verb to complete the sentence.**

1. Maria non _____ (sa/conosce) ancora nuotare (*yet*).

2. No _____ (so/conosco) questo computer.

3. _____ (sai/conosci) l'Australia?

4. _____ (conoscono/sanno) il numero di telefono di Luigi?

5. Carlo non _____ (conosce/sa) il dottore.

To know is knowing you know nothing

ANSWER KEY ?≡

Practice. 1.1

A. 1. sappiamo 2. sai 3. sapete 4. sa 5. so 6. sa 7. sanno 8. sa

Practice. 2.1

A. 1. conoscono 2. conosce 3. conoscete 4. conosciamo 5. conosco 6. conosce 7. conosci 8. conosce

B. 1. conosce 2. sapete 3. sanno 4. sa 5. conosce 6. conosci 7. so 8. conoscete/conoscete

C. 1. conosco 2. sappiamo 3. conoscete 4. conosce 5. sai 6. sanno 7. conosco 8. conosce 9. sanno

D. 1. X 2. X 3. X 4. X 5. a 6. a 7. a

Practice. 3.1

A. 1. Novak Djokovic sa giocare a tennis 2. LeBron James sa giocare a pallacanestro 3. Tiger Woods sa giocare a golf 4. J. K. Rowling sa romanzi 5. Lionel Messi e Cristiano Ronaldo sanno giocare a calcio 6. Taylor Swift sa cantare 7. Michael Phelps sa nuotare 8. Shakira sa ballare 9. Meryl Streep sa recitare 10. Simon Biles sa fare ginnastica artistica

B. 1. Sherlock Holmes conosce Watson 2. Ashton Kutcher conosce Mila Kunis 3. Rhett Butler conosce Scarlett O'Hara 4. Chris Martin conosce Dakota Johnson 5. David Beckham conosce Victoria Beckham 6. Adamo conosce Eva 7. Justin Bieber conosce Hailey Bieber

C. 1. Io conosco il professor Blanco 2. Mia sorella e io conosciamo la madre di Juan 3. Maria e Luigi conoscono Sergio 4. Voi conoscete il direttore dell'area commerciale 5. Tu conosci la zia Julia 6. Carlos conosce la zia Julia 7. Martino e Elena conoscono la zia Julia.

D. 1. Io so la verità 2. Lei conosce Maria 3. Loro sanno nuotare 4. Pietro e Elena conoscono New York 5. Conosciamo/Sappiamo la risposta 6. Conosciamo lo studente 7. Tu sai il mio nome 8. Lui conosce/sa la verità 9. Il cane conosce Juan 10. So suonare il pianoforte 11. Conosciamo l'università

E. 1. sa 2. conosco 3. conosci 4. sanno 5. conosce

LESSON 09

SPEAKING OF WHICH

THE INDICATIVE MOOD: PRESENT TENSE OF **PARLARE** (*TO SPEAK*) – **MANGIARE** (*TO EAT*) – **VIVERE** (*TO LIVE*)

Verbs in Italian ending in **-are, -ere,** and **-ire** are called *regular verbs* because they all follow a regular pattern. As we've discussed, Italian verbs change according to the person and the number of the subject. They're much simpler to modify when we're dealing with regular verbs!

 # VERBS ENDING IN -ARE

The -are verbs follow the pattern of **parlare.** Below are some of them:

lavorare	[lah-voh-rah-reh]	*to work*
studiare	[stoo-dyah-reh]	*to study*

guardare	[gwahr-dah-reh]	*to look*
arrivare	[ahr-ree-vah-reh]	*to arrive*
cercare	[chehr-kah-reh]	*to look for*
insegnare	[een-seh-nyah-reh]	*to teach*
comprare	[kohm-prah-reh]	*to buy*
necessitare	[neh-chehs-see-tah-reh]	*to need*
pagare	[pah-gah-reh]	*to pay*
ritornare	[reeh-tohr-nah-reh]	*to return (to a place)*
mangiare	[mahn-gyah-reh]	*To eat*
preparare	[preh-pah-rah-reh]	*to prepare*
riparare	[ree-pah-rah-reh]	*to fix*
viaggiare	[vee-ahj-jah-reh]	*to travel*
spiegare	[spee-eh-gah-reh]	*to explain*

The present tense form of verbs ending in **-are** is conjugated by removing the infinitive **-are** ending and replacing it with an ending corresponding to the person that is performing the action of the verb. See below:

Speak Abroad
Academy

---

parlare *to speak*

io (*I*)	**parlo**	noi (*we*)	**parliamo**
tu (*you*)	**parli**	voi (*you*)	**parlate**
egli/lui (*he*)		essi (*they*)	
ella/lei (*she*)	**parla**	esse (*they*)	**parlano**
esso (*it*)		loro (*they*)	

Lei/Voi (*You – formal*) **parla/parlate**

1.1.   Practice

Reading Comprehension

A. Check this dialogue. Can you translate what Luisa, and the grocer are saying?

Dal fruttivendolo

LUISA: Buongiorno, ha delle banane?

FRUTTIVENDLO: Buongiorno. Sì, ce l'ho le banane.

LUISA: Ah, quanto costano?

FRUTTIVENDOLO: Costano 20 euro al chilo.

LUISA: Ottimo. Ne compro due chili.

FRUTTIVENDOLO: D'accordo. Ecco a Lei.

LUISA: Tante grazie. Arrivederci.

Glossary:

Avere: *to have*

Quanto costa...?: *how much are...?*

Chilo: *kilogram*

Ecco a Lei: *Here you are*

Vocabulary: the house

Here are some helpful vocabulary words that you'll need to know. They all refer to various parts of the house and some common items that you'll find in them.

Speak Abroad
Academy

il salotto	[eel sah-loht-toh]	*the living room*
la sala da pranzo	[lah sah-lah dah prahn-tsoh]	*the dining room*
la cucina	[lah kooh-chee-nah]	*the kitchen*
la tazza	[lah taht-tsah]	*the cup*
il bicchiere	[eel beek-kyeh-reh]	*the glass*
Il frigorifero	[eel free-goh-ree-feh-roh]	*the refrigerator*
Il forno	[eel fohr-noh]	*the oven*
la camera da letto	[lah kah-meh-rah dah leht-toh]	*the bedroom*
il garage	[eel gah-rah-djeh]	*the garage*
le scale	[leh skah-leh]	the stairs
il bagno	[eel bah-nyoh]	*the bathroom*
lo specchio	[loh spehk-kyoh]	*the mirror*
il tetto	[eel teht-toh]	*the roof*

B. Give the corresponding subject pronouns. Example: ritornate <u>voi</u>

1. insegno _____
2. cantiamo _____
3. studiano _____

4. paga _____
5. desidero _____
6. cerca _____

7. compra _____

8. parlate _____

9. lavorano _____

10. ritorni _____

C. In biblioteca

Marco sta in biblioteca. Studia per un esame di matematica. L'esame è domani (*tomorrow*). Ha tanti libri da leggere. Marco sta in ansia. Ha bisogno di studiare tanto. L'esame è molto difficile.

Confirm whether these statements are true (**vero**) or false (**falso**), based on the information in the paragraph above.

1. Marco è un professore _____

2. Marco studia a (*his*) casa _____

3. Marco ha un esame domani _____

4. L'esame è molto facile _____

A. Answer these questions of conjugating the verbs ending in -ar to match the person performing the action.

1. Mio padre _____ (lavorare) dal lunedì al venerdì.

2. I tuoi figli _____ (guardare) troppa televisione.

3. Voi _____ (cercare) scarpe buone.

4. La professoressa Oliva _____ (insegnare) in tre classi.

5. _____ (io/comprare) frutta e verdura tutte le settimane.

6. Teresa e Pietro _____ (viaggiare) in treno al lavoro.

7. Noi _____ (spiegare) ai nostri figli come comportarsi (*how to behave*).

8. Il signor Romanelli _____ (riparare) borse.

E. Fill in the blanks with the correct verb form:

Infinitive	parlare	insegnare	lavorare	guardare
io		insegno		
tu	parli			guardi
egli/ella/ lui/lei/Lei			lavora	
noi	parliamo			guardiamo
voi			lavorate	
esse/essi/loro		insegnano		

2 VERBS ENDING IN -ERE

The **-ere** verbs follow the pattern of **bere.** Below are some of them:

apprendere	[ahp-prehn-deh-re]	*to learn*
prendere	[prehn-deh-reh]	*to take/to drink*
bere	[beh-reh]	*to drink*
comprendere	[kohm-prehn-deh-reh]	*to understand*

Speaking of which

credere	[kreh-deh-reh]	*to think to believe in*
dovere (+ infinito)	[doh-veh-reh]	*should, must, ought to (do something)*
leggere	[lehj-jeh-reh]	*to read*
vendere	[vehn-deh-reh]	*to sell*
mettere	[meht-teh-reh]	*to put in*
prendere	[prehn-deh-reh]	to turn on
correre	[kohr-reh-ehr]	*to run*
rompere	[rohm-peh-reh]	*to break*

You'll notice that all these verbs end in **-ere**! When we're speaking in the present tense, we remove the **-ere** from verbs like the ones in the table above, and we add a new ending depending on the pronoun that goes before it. In other words, the ending of the word changes depending on who and how many people are being referred to.

Refer to the diagram box below for the rules on how to modify the endings of these verbs for each pronoun.

---

bere *to eat*

io (*I*)	**bev-o**	noi (*we*)	**bev-iamo**
tu (*you*)	**bev-i**	voi (*you*)	**bev-ete**
egli/lui (*he*)		essi (*they*)	
ella/lei (*she*)	**bev-e**	esse (*they*)	**bev-ono**
esso (*it*)		loro (*they*)	
Lei/Voi (*You – formal*)			**beve/bevete**

Anche is an adverb. It means 'as well,' 'too,' or 'also.'

Reading Comprehension

Al ristorante

Stiamo al ristorante "Carlitos". Siamo quindici persone. Lavoriamo tutti insieme nello stesso ufficio. Abbiamo un tavolo grande. La carne di questo ristorante è molto deliziosa. Ci sono anche pollo e pesce. È tutto squisito. Il cameriere prende l'ordinazione e torna con il cibo. Mangiamo e beviamo molto bene.

Speaking of which

— Glossary: —

in: in

tutti: all

insieme: together

lo stesso: the same

colleghi: coworkers

molto bene: very well

carne: meat

di: of

questo: this

anche: also

pollo: chicken

pesce: fish

tutto: everything

cameriere: waiter

ordinazione: order

con: with

A. Answer the following questions in this text.

Example: La carne di questo ristorante è cattiva? <u>No, la carne di questo ristorante è deliziosa.</u>

1. Siete venti persone a tavola? _____

2. Lavorate tutti allo stesso ufficio? _____

3. Avete pollo e pesce? _____

4. Avete un tavolo piccolo? _____

B. Complete these sentences with the appropriate form of the right verb. Use each verb once.

bere - comprendere - prendere - leggere - correre - apprendere - vendere

1. Il bambino non _____ la lezione.

2. Luigi e Maria _____ la televisione.

3. La ragazza _____ al collegio per (*to*) arrivare tardi (*late*).

4. Noi _____ la casa e compriamo un appartamento.

5. Voi _____ in quel (*that*) ristorante eccellente.

Speaking of which

6. Tu e io _____ molta acqua.

7. Tutte le domeniche _____ (io) il giornale.

8. Tutti i giorni _____ (tu) qualcosa.

C. Fill in the blanks with the correct verb form:

Infinito	bere	vendere	credere	apprendere
io	bevo			apprendo
tu		vendi		
egli/ella/				
lui/lei			credi	
noi	mangiamo			apprendiamo
voi		vendete		
esse/essi/loro			credono	

3 VERBS ENDING IN -IRE

The **-ire** verbs follow the pattern of **aprire.** Below are some of them:

aprire	[ah-pree-reh]	*to open*
dormire	[dohr-mee-reh]	*to write*
gradire	[grah-dee-reh]	*to receive*
concepire	[kohn-chee-pee-reh]	*to share*
spedire	[speh-dee-reh]	*to decide*
partire	[pahr-tee-reh]	*to describe*
preferire	[preh-feh-ree-reh]	*to discuss*
salire	[sah-lee-reh]	*to go up*
soffrire	[sohf-free-reh]	*to suffer*

We talked about how to modify verbs ending in **-ere**, but what about verbs that end in **-ire**? To use these verbs in the present tense, we remove the **-ir** ending and change it according to the subject, just like the other verbs. See below for how to modify these verbs.

---

partire *to live*

io (*I*)	**parto**	noi (*we*)	**partiamo**
tu (*you*)	**parti**	voi (*you*)	**partite**
egli/lui (*he*)		essi (*they*)	
ella/lei (*she*)	**parte**	esse (*they*)	**partono**
esso (*it*)		loro (*they*)	
Lei/Voi (*You – formal*)	**parte/partite**		

TIP

In English, a verb must have an expressed subject (**he** eats spaghetti). In Italian, 'he' or 'she' is not always necessary. Why? Because it's obvious from the verb who you are referring to. People tend to omit using subject pronouns unless you want to clarify who's doing the action or place emphasis on it.

─────── **Common Mistake:** ───────

You might feel it's natural to add a pronoun in Italian but think twice before you do it. Most of the time, your verbs will do the work for you!

Don't say, **Io voglio un caffè** (*I want a coffee*)X Say instead, Voglio un caffè✓

Don't say, **Noi vogliamo andare in spiaggia domani** (*We want to go to the beach tomorrow*) X Say instead, **Vogliamo andare in spiaggia domani** ✓

3.1. Practice

A. Complete these sentences with the appropriate form of the correct verbs listed. Use each verb once.

dormire – salire – spedire - sentire - gradire - seguire - preferire - aprire

1.   I bambini _____ le caramelle (*candy*).

2.   Tutti gli studenti _____ le scale per (*for*) la lezione di matematica.

3.   Marco _____ per la città; Maria _____ per la campagna (*country*)

4.   Io _____ la porta (*door*).

5.   Tu _____ i tuoi amici in casa tua

6.   Voi _____ lettere (*letters*) ai vostri genitori.

7.   Noi _____ il notiziario (*the news*) con mio marito (*husband*).

8.   Tu _____ studiare lo spagnolo.

B. Fill in the blanks with the correct verb form:

Infinito	spedire	dormire	aprire	salire
io	scrivo			salgo
tu		dormi		
egli/ella/ lui/lei			apre	
noi	scriviamo			saliamo
voi		dormite		
esse/essi/loro			aprono	

ANSWER KEY

Practice. 1.1

A.   Reading Comprehension

B.   At the Grocer's

LUISA: Good morning, do you have bananas?

GROCER: Good morning. Yes, I do have bananas.

LUISA: Oh, how much are they?

GROCER: They are 20 pesos for a kilogram.

LUISA: Very well. I need to buy two kilograms.

GROCER: Ok. Here you are.

LUISA: Thank you very much. Goodbye.

Practice. 1.2

A. 1. io 2. noi 3. voi/loro 4. egli/ella/Lei 5. io 6. tu 7. lui/lei/Lei 8. voi 9. loro/voi 10. tu

B. 1. falso 2. falso 3. vero 4. falso

C. 1. lavora 2. guardano 3. cercate 4. insegna 5. compro 6. viaggiano 7. spieghiamo 8. ripara

D.

Infinito	parlare	insegnare	lavorare	guardare
io	parlo	insegno	lavoro	guardo
tu	parli	insegni	lavori	guardi
egli/ella/Lei	parla	insegna	lavora	guarda
noi	parliamo	insegniamo	lavoriamo	guardiamo
voi	parlate	insegniate	lavorate	guardate
esse/essi/loro	parlano	insegnano	lavorano	guardano

Practice. 2.1

A. 1. No, sono quindici persone al tavolo. 2. Sì, lavorano tutti nello stesso ufficio. 3. Sì, hanno pollo e pesce. 4. No, hanno un tavolo grande.

B. 1. comprende 2. prendono 3. corre 4. vendiamo 5. mangiate 6. beviamo 7. leggo 8. apprendi

C.

Infinito	mangiare	vendere	credere	apprendere
io	mangio	vendo	credo	apprendo
tu	mangi	vendi	credi	apprendi
egli/ella lui/lei	mangia	vende	crede	apprende
noi	mangiamo	vendiamo	crediamo	apprendiamo
voi	mangiate	vendete	credete	apprendete
esse/essi/loro	mangiano	vendono	credono	apprendono

Practice. 3.1

A. 1. condividono 2. salgono 3. vive... vive 4. apro 5. ricevi 6. scrivi 7. discutiamo 8. decidi

B.

Infinitive	partire	spedire	abrire	salire
io	parto	spedisco	apro	salgo
tu	parti	spedisci	apri	sali
egli/ella/ lui/lei	parte	spedisce	apre	sale
noi	partiamo	spediamo	apriamo	saliamo
voi	partite	spedite	aprite	salite
esse/essi/loro	partono	spediscono	aprono	salgono

LESSON 10

WHAT TIME IS IT?

Navigating everyday life would be pretty hard without the ability to ask for and express the time. In this lesson, we'll go over everything you need to know to understand this crucial component of language.

1 WHAT TIME IS IT?

To ask, 'what time is it?' in Italian, you say **Che ora è?**

If it's one o'clock, the response will be È l'una.

And if it's a number higher than one, you'll phrase it as **sono le due** or **sono le tre**, and so on. As you can see, we're using è again, which is both the singular and plural third-person form of the verb **essere**.

È l'una	*It's one o'clock*
Sono le due	*It's two o'clock*
Sono le quattro	*It's four o'clock*
Sono le dieci	*It's ten o'clock*

If you want to say "sharp" or "exactly," Italian uses **esattamente** or **in punto**.

Sono le undici in punto	*It's eleven o'clock sharp*
Sono le sei in punto	*It's six o'clock sharp*
Sono le otto in punto	*It's sharp eight o'clock*

If, instead, your kind of hesitant about the time, you can say **più o meno** (*about*).

Sono più o meno le nove	*It's about nine o'clock*
È l'una circa	*It's about one o'clock*

If you want to say it's half past the hour, use **e mezza** or è trenta. For example, **sono le otto e mezza** (*it's eight thirty*).

Sono le dodici e mezza	*It's twelve thirty*
Sono le dieci e trenta	*It's ten thirty*
Sono le quattro e mezza	*It's four thirty*

To indicate that it's a number past the hour, use **e + number of minutes**: For example, **sono le sette e venti** (it's 7:20).

Sono le due e cinque	*It's 2:05*
Sono le sei e dieci	*It's 6:10*

What time is it?

Sono le otto e venti   *It's 8:20*

È l'una e venticinque   *It's 1:25*

And to say it's a number to the hour, say **meno + number of minutes**. For example, **sono le tre meno venti** (it's twenty to three).

Sono le nove meno dieci   *It's 8:50*

È l'una meno venti   *It's 12:40*

Sono le quattro meno cinque   *It's 3:55*

Sono le dodici meno venticinque   *It's 11:35*

What about fifteen minutes past the hour?

In Italian, when it's a quarter after the hour, you say **e un quarto** (*quarter*) or **e quindici** (*fifteen*).

Sono le sette e un quarto
= It's 7:15

Sono le quattro e un quarto
= It's 6:15

Sono le sei e un quarto
= It's 4:15

And when it's fifteen minutes before the hour, in Italiano you say **meno un quarto** or, less frequently, **meno quindici**.

Sono le otto meno un quarto	*It's 7:45*
Sono le tre meno un quarto	*It's 2:45*
È l'una meno un quarto	*It's 12:45*

Another way of expressing the time before the hour is saying the **number of minutes + per + l'ora** (the hour). For example: **Sono dieci alle due**.

Sono venti alle quattro	*It's twenty minutes to four o'clock*
Sono dieci all'una	*It's ten minutes to one o'clock*
Sono venticinque alle dodici	*It's twenty-five minutes to twelve o'clock*

Here are more examples:

È l'una

Sono le undici

Sono le sei

È l'una meno dieci

Sono le otto e mezza

Sono le sette e venti

1.1.   Practice

1   3

2   4

Che ora è? State in words what time it is on each clock.

1. _____

2. _____

3. _____

4. _____

B. Che ora è?

1.   3:45: _____

2.   11:00: _____

3.   1:30: _____

4.   6:45: _____

5.   8:15: _____

6.   9:20: _____

C. State what time it is and what it's time for. Example: Mezzogiorno. → Son las Sono le dodici. È ora di pranzo.

Some activities you might use are: **cenare** (*have dinner*) - **camminare - lavorare – guardare la televisioner - correre - tornare a casa – andare a prendere i miei figli** (*pick my kids up*) - **mangiare** -

1.   8:00: _____

2.   10:00: _____

3.   1:15: _____

4.   4:30: _____

5.   6:00 _____

6.   8:00 _____

D. At what time do we travel to... Form sentences according to the cues. **Example: Londra / 8:15 → <u>A che ora partiamo per Londra? Alle otto e un quarto.</u>**

1.   Parigi /12.00

2.   Madrid / 1:00

3.   Praga / 5:30

4.   Lima / 9:15

5.   Buenos Aires / 8:45

6.   Washington / 5:45

2 ¿AT WHAT TIME IS...?

To indicate at what time something is happening, in Italian you ask, "**A che ora è...?**" (*"At what time is...?"*). And the answer is, "**Al/alle...**" (*At...*) or "È al/alle..." (*"It's at..."*)

A che ora è la cena?	*At what time is dinner?*
È l'una	*It's at one*

A che ora è il programma?	*At what time is the program?*
Sono le tre.	*It's at three*

TIP

Note that **cibo/cena/pranzo** can mean *food*, but it can also mean *dinner* or the *moment you eat.*

What about references to the time of day? Italian also specifies whether something happens in the morning, at noon, in the afternoon, or at night.

del mattino	*of the morning: a.m.*
di mezzogiorno	*of noon: p.m.*
del pomeriggio	*of the afternoon: p.m.*
della sera	*of the night: p.m.*
di mezzanotte	*of midnight: a.m.*

Sono le tre del mattino	*It's at three in the morning (3:00 a.m.)*
Sono le otto di sera	*It's at eight in the evening ((8:00 p.m.)*
È mezzogiorno	*It's at twelve noon (12:00 p.m.)*
È mezzanotte	*It's at twelve midnight (12:00 a.m.)*

Vocabolario: social events

la festa	[lah feh-stah]	*the party*
la lezione	[lah leh-tsyoh-neh]	*the class*
la riunione	[lah ryoo-nyoh-neh]	*the meeting*
il pranzo	[eel prahn-tsoh]	*the lunch meeting*
l'appuntamento	[lahp-poohn-tah-mehn-toh]	*the appointment*
l'evento	[leh-vehn-toh]	*the event*

2.1.   Practice

In everyday language, you can omit the verb è when you're **answering** a time that something happens; for example, **A che ora è la cena?** The answer would be **Alle otto di sera.**

A. Respond to some more questions by spelling out the numbers and including the time indicated. You can add "del mattino", "del pomeriggio" to make it more complete! **Example: A che ora è la cena? Alle tre del pomeriggio.**

1.   A che ora è il pranzo? (12:00 p.m.) _____

2.   A che ora è l'appuntamento? (4:00 p.m.) _____

3.   A che ora è la tua lezione? (8:00 a.m.) _____

4.   A che ora è la riunione? (11:00 a.m.) _____

5.   A che ora è la festa? (12:00 a.m.) _____

6.   A che ora è l'evento? (3:00 p.m.) _____

B. Translate these expressions:

1.　It's eleven o'clock sharp: _____

2.　It's eight thirty: _____

3.　It's eight in the morning: _____

4.　It's about three o'clock in the afternoon: _____

5.　It's ten thirty: _____

6.　It's five thirty: _____

7.　It's seven twenty: _____

8.　It's twenty to one: _____

9.　It's five to two: _____

10.　It's twenty-five to two: _____

11.　It's eight fifteen: _____

12.　It's a quarter to four: _____

3　THE DAYS OF THE WEEK

lunedì	[loo-neh-dee]	Monday
martedì	[mahr-teh-dee]	Tuesday
mercoledì	[mehr-koh-leh-dee]	Wednesday
giovedì	[joh-veh-dee]	Thursday
venerdì	[veh-nehr-dee]	Friday

sabato	[sah-bah-toh]	*Saturday*
domenica	[doh-meh-nee-kah]	*Sunday*

If you want to say you do something on a certain day every week, you say: **Lavoro il lunedì**
(*I work on Mondays*)**.**

If you want to say you do something from one day to another, you say: **Lavoro dal lunedì al venerdì**
(*I work from Monday to Friday*)

If you want to say you do something on the weekends, you say: **Gioco a tennis nei fine settimana**
(*I play tennis on the weekends*).

Reading Comprehension

Listen to the song **Di nuovo lunedì** (*Lunes otra vez) (Monday, again*), by Argentine singer,
songwriter, and musician Charlie García. It brings to mind the Monday blues, prevalent in every
culture around the globe. Try to follow the lyrics while you do.

https://www.youtube.com/watch?v=VF4WhZoTz9c

Di nuovo lunedì	**Monday, again**
Di nuovo lunedì sopra la città.	*Monday again over the city.*
La gente che vedi in solitudine.	*The people you see live in solitude.*
Sul bosco grigio vedo morire il sole	*On the gray forest, I see the sun dying*
Che domani sul viale sorgerà.	*that tomorrow will shine again on the avenue.*

Strade incolori, vestite di grigio.	*Colourless roads, dressed in gray.*
Dalla mia finestra vedo il tappeto verde	*From my window I see the green carpet*
di un parco che domani morirà,	*of a park that will die tomorrow,*
e morto il verde solo il ferro crescerà	*and once the green dies, only iron will prevail.*

Vecchie donne in un angolo chiedono pane;	*Old women in the corner beg for bread;*
negli uffici, la morte della società.	*in the offices, the death of society.*
Oggi tutti ciechi, che non sanno guardare	*Everyone is blind today, not knowing how to see*
l'orrida risata della pallida città.	*the horrid laughter of the pale city.*

Di nuovo lunedì sopra la città.	*Monday again over the city.*
La gente che vedi in solitudine.	*The people you see live in solitude.*
Sarà sempre uguale, mai cambierà.	*It will always be the same, it will never change*
Lunedì è il giorno triste e grigio di solitudine.	*Monday is the sad and gray day of solitude.*

3.1. Practice

A. Answer these questions about the song ***Lunedì, ancora***:

1. Di che colore è il lunedì per questo autore? _____

2.   Com'è il lunedì? _____

3.   Come vive la gente? (*How do people live?*)_____

4.   Cosa non sanno fare i ciechi (*blind people*)? _____

B. Look at Monica's schedule and answer the questions below:

	LUNEDÌ	MARTEDÌ	MERCOLEDÌ	GIOVEDÌ	VENERDÌ	SABATO	DOMENICA
9:15	pagare bollette			prendere café con Elena			
10:30	studiare	studiare	studiare	studiare	studiare	giocare a tennis	giocare a golf
11:45							
4:15	prendere bambini a scuola	prendere bambini a scuola	prendere bambini a scuola	prendere bambini a scuola	prendere bambini a scuola		
6:45	cucinare	cucinare	cucinare	cucinare	cucinare	ristorante	ordinare pizza (order pizza)
8:15	cenare	cenare	cenare	cenare	cenare		

1.   A che ora Monica prende i figli a scuola? _____

2.   A che ora paga le bollette? _____

3.   A che ora studia? _____

4.   Quando studia? _____

5.   Quando gioca a tennis? _____

6.   Quando gioca a golf? _____

4 THE MONTHS OF THE YEAR

gennaio	[jehn-nah-yoh]	*January*
febbraio	[fehb-brah-yoh]	*February*
marzo	[mahr-tsoh]	*March*
aprile	[ah-pree-leh]	*April*
maggio	[mahj-joh]	*May*
giugno	[joo-nyoh]	*June*
luglio	[looh-lyoh]	*July*
agosto	[ah-goh-stoh]	*August*
settembre	[seht-tehm-breh]	*September*
ottobre	[oht-toh-breh]	*October*
novembre	[noh-vehm-breh]	*November*
dicembre	[dee-chehm-breh]	*December*

> Now that we're learning about time, the adverb **quando?** (*when*) is a useful word to know.

Other period expressions:

Che giorno è oggi?	*What is today's date?*
Oggi è il 18 agosto.	*Today is August 18.*
Oggi è il primo di maggio.	*Today is May 1st.*
Il mio compleanno è il 2 giugno.	*My birthday is June 2.*
La festa è l'8 ottobre.	*The party is October 8.*

When it's the first day of the month, you should use the ordinal number **primo**. After that, cardinal numbers (**due, tre, quattro**, and so on) should be used.

> Remember to use the article **il** before the date when you're stating when an event takes place: **La riunione è per il 7 novembre** (*the meeting is on November 7*).

> The months of the year and the days of the week are not capitalized in Italian: **oggi è lunedì, 2 marzo**.

—————— Common Error: ——————

When you want to say, "Today is Thursday," don't say **Oggi è il giovedì** X

Say, instead, **Oggi è giovedì** (omit the **il**). ✔

TIP

On the other hand, if you want to state when a specific event takes place, always use **il**. For example:

Natale è **il** 25 dicembre.

Capodanno è **il** primo gennaio.

Il mio compleanno è **il** 4 agosto.

L'indipendenza degli Stati Uniti è **il** 4 luglio.

The year is divided into seasons: summer (estate), fall or autumn (autunno), winter (inverno), and spring (primavera).

l'estate	**giugno**	**l'autunno**	**settembre**
	luglio		**ottobre**
	agosto		**novembre**

la primavera	**marzo**	**l'inverno**	**dicembre**
	aprile		**gennaio**
	maggio		**febbraio**

4.1. Practice

A. State when these events take place:

1. Quando è il tuo compleanno (birthday)? _____

2. Quando si celebra l'indipendenza degli Stati Uniti? _____

3. Quando inizia (starts) l'estate in Europa? _____

4. Quando è Natale (Christmas)? _____

5. Quando è Capodanno (New Year's)? _____

B. Link the words with the season of the year and write a sentence. **Example: neve → inverno. In inverno c'è neve or freddo → inverno. In inverno fa freddo.**

Seasons: primavera - estate - autunno - inverno

1. Fiori → _____

2. Sole → _____

3. Foglie secche (dry leaves) → _____

4. Caldo → _____

5. Vento → _____

6. Ghiaccio (ice) → _____

ANSWER KEY

Practice. 1.1.

A. 1. Sono le nove e dieci 2. Sono le sei e cinque 3. Sono le sette e venticinque 4. Sono le dodici e un quarto

B. 1. Sono le quattro meno un quarto 2. Sono le undici in punto 3. È l'una e mezza 4. Sono le sette meno un quarto 5. Sono le otto e un quarto 6. Sono le nove e venti

C. 1. Sono le otto. È ora di lavorare. 2. Sono le dieci. È ora di passeggiare 3. È l'una e un quarto. È ora di pranzare. 4. Sono le quattro e mezza. È ora di ritornare a casa. 5. Sono le sei. È ora di andare a prendere i miei figli. 6. Sono le otto. È ora di cenare.

D. 1. A che ora partiamo per Parigi? Alle dodici in punto. 2. A che ora partiamo per Madrid? All'una in punto. 3. A che ora partiamo per Praga? Alle cinque e mezza. 4. A che ora partiamo per Lima? Alle nove e un quarto. 5. A che ora partiamo per Buenos Aires? Alle nove meno un quarto. A che ora partiamo per Washington? Alle sei meno un quarto.

Practice. 2.1

A. 1. È mezzogiorno. 2. Sono le quattro del pomeriggio. 3. Sono le otto del mattino. 4. Sono le undici di mattina. 5. È mezzanotte. 6. Sono le tre del pomeriggio.

B. 1. Sono le undici in punto. 2. Sono le otto e mezza. 3. Sono le otto del mattino. 4. Sono più o meno le tre del pomeriggio. 5. Sono le dieci e mezza 6. Sono le cinque e mezza. 7. Sono le sette e venti. 8. È l'una meno venti. 9. Sono le due meno cinque. 10. Sono le due meno venticinque. 11. Sono le otto e un quarto. 12. Sono le quattro meno un quarto.

Practice. 3.1

A. 1. Il lunedì è grigio. 2. Il lunedì è triste 3. La gente vive in solitudine 4. Non sanno guardare.

B. 1. Alle quattro e un quarto. 2. Alle nove e un quarto. 3. Alle dieci e mezza. 4. Dal lunedì al venerdì. 5. I sabato 6. Le domeniche.

Practice. 4.1

A. A. 1. Il mio compleanno è il (answer varies) 2. L'indipendenza degli Stati Uniti si celebra il 4 luglio 3. L'estate inizia il 21 giugno in Europa 4. Natale è il 25 dicembre 5. Capodanno è il 1° gennaio.

B. B. 1. Fiori → primavera. In primavera ci sono i fiori. 2. Sole → estate. In estate c'è il sole. 3. Foglie secche → autunno. In autunno ci sono le foglie secche. 4. Caldo → estate. In estate fa caldo. 5. vento → autunno. In autunno c'è vento. 6. Ghiaccio → inverno. In inverno c'è ghiaccio.

YES, SIR; NO, SIR

AFFIRMATIVE AND NEGATIVE SENTENCES

Affirmative and negative sentences are an important part of everyday conversations. When we use an affirmative sentence, we're saying something *is* or that something *did* happen. It's a positive statement. On the other hand, negative sentences express that something is *not* or that something *didn't* happen. It's the opposite of an affirmative sentence.

An affirmative sentence would be 'the cat is blue.' In retort to this, a negative sentence would be 'the cat is not blue.'

So, how do we express these positive and negative sentences in Italian?

1 AFFIRMATIVE AND NEGATIVE SENTENCES

We've covered a lot of affirmative sentences already in the book. But let's give you a refresher on how to write these sentences.

When constructing an affirmative sentence in Italian, the subject (the noun) usually goes at the beginning of the sentence. After the noun, we add the verb. We end up with a sentence such as:

Il cane salta (*The dog jumps*)

There are also words that, by default, are affirmative words.

In Italian, they are:

qualcosa	*something*
qualcuno	*someone*
alcun, alcuno, alcuna	*one, a, an, any*
alcuni, alcune	*some, any*
a volte, alcune volte	*sometimes*
sempre	*always*
anche	*also / too / as well*

Let's go back to the sentence about the dog jumping. What if we wanted to turn this sentence into a negative one and state that the dog is *not* jumping?

To do so, we'd add the word **non** right after the noun and before the verb.

Il cane non salta (*The dog does not jump*)

Just as there are affirmative words, there are also inherently negative words.

Negative words are:

no	*no*
né	*neither / nor*
niente	*nothing*
nessuno	*no one / nobody*
mai	*never*
nessuno	*not one*
mai	*never*

Do you know what a double negative is? We use them in English all the time. They're technically not grammatically correct to use in any language, but they're extremely common in everyday, informal speech.

A double negative sentence occurs when we combine two negative words in the same sentence. Like, for example, 'She didn't do nothing' or 'I didn't see nobody.' They're confusing because the technical meaning is different from their intended meaning. When someone says, 'She didn't do nothing' they *mean* to emphasize that 'She didn't do anything.'

Yes, sir; no, sir

To construct a double negative sentence in Italian, you add a negative word before *and* after the main verb in a sentence. The first word is usually 'non.' For example:

Lei non ha niente (*She doesn't have nothing*)

In other words, it's arranged as subject + **non** + verb + **nada.**

Let's take a look at the following negative and double negative sentences:

La bambina non mangia niente	*The girl doesn't eat nothing*
Non so niente	*I know nothing*
Il bambino non capisce niente	*The boy doesn't understand nothing.*

Luigi non compra niente dal fruttivendolo *Luis buys nothing in the fruit store/Luis doesn't buy anything in the fruit store.*

Non abbiamo bisogno di niente *We need nothing/We don't need anything.*

> How do you translate a sentence like **The man doesn't speak Spanish?** Well, in Italian there is no equivalent for the English word *do* or *does* in negative sentences. You simply say **L'uomo non parla spagnolo**.

The negative words you use to form **double negative sentences** in Italian are:

1.   Adverbs of denial (see below)

2.   Indefinite pronouns ('anything,' 'something,' etc.)

Adverbs of Denial

no/non	no - not
né	nor - neither
mai	never
neanche/nemmeno	neither
mai	never, ever

The order of words in the sentence es **non + verb + adverb of denial + complement**

Examples:

- ➲ **Non** mi piace **n**é il nuoto né il tennis: *I don't like swimming or tennis*

- ➲ Maria **non** mangia **né** verdura né frutta: *Maria doesn't eat vegetables or fruits*

- ➲ **Non** vado **mai** al ristorante: *I never go to a restaurant*

- ➲ Luigi **non** va **mai** a trovare Elena: *Luis never visits Elena*

Indefinite Pronouns

The other way to create double negative sentences in Italian is with **indefinite pronouns**. They're 'indefinite' because they're vague about who they are referring to, e.g., 'someone' or 'anyone.' They can also be negative like 'no one' or 'nothing.'

The order is the same as with adverbs of denial: **no + verb + indefinite pronoun + complement**

These are negative indefinite pronouns:

nessuno	*no one / nobody*
niente	*nothing / anything*
nessuno / nessuna	*any / none / anyone / no one*

Examples:

- **Non** c'è **niente** da mangiare in casa: *There is nothing to eat in the house*
- **Non** capisco **niente** di tedesco: *I don't understand any German*
- **Non** ha bisogno di **nessuno**: *He/she doesn't need any of them*
- **Non** c'è **nessuno** in città: *There is no one in the city*

1.1. Practice

Reading Comprehension

Check this dialogue out:

Teresa va a cena dalla sua amica Isabella, ma non le importa di mangiare niente.

Isabella: Vuoi qualcosa da mangiare?	*Do you want something to eat?*
Teresa: **No**, grazie. **Non** voglio mangiare **niente**.	*No, thank you. I won't eat anything.*
Isabella: E qualcosa da bere?	*And something to drink?*
Teresa: **Non** voglio **neanche** da bere	*I won't drink anything either.*
Isabella: Davvero **non** vuoi **niente**?	*You really don't want anything?*
Teresa: **Non** mangio **mai** a cena.	*I never have anything for dinner.*
Isabella: **Non** mangi **mai** la sera?	*You never eat anything at night?*
Teresa: **No.** Dormo meglio.	*No. I sleep better.*

Notice that when the adverbs or pronouns of denial are placed directly **before** the first verb, you don't need the double negative: **Non mangio mai la sera.**

Yes, sir; no, sir

Nessuno/nessuna is an adjective. It must concur in number and gender with the noun it modifies: **Non ha nessuna camera da letto**.

When **nessuno** is before a masculine singular noun, it shortens to **nessun**.

Nessuno/a is not used in the plural unless it accompanies a noun that is always in the plural, like **vacanze** (vacations): **Non hanno bisogno di vacanze.**

If **nessuno/a** precedes the noun, you don't need a **non**: **Nessuna persona capisce il latino.**

─── Remember: ───

the opposite of **nessuno** (*no one*) is **qualcuno** (*someone / some*)

A. Answer these questions about the dialogue above:

1. Teresa vuole mangiare qualcosa? _____

2. Teresa vuole bere qualcosa? _____

3. Teresa desidera qualcosa? _____

4. Teresa cena mai la sera? _____

B. Give the opposite of the following:

1.   qualcosa _____ 2. qualcuno _____ 3. qualcuno

_____ 4. sempre _____ 5. anche _____ 6. niente

_____ 7. nessuno _____ 8. nessuno _____ 9. mai

_____ 10. neanche _____

C. Translate the following using **alcun, alcuno, alcuna, qualche, del/della** (*one, a, an, any*), **alcuni, alcune** (*some, any*), and **nessun, nessuno, nessuna** (*none, no one*). **Example: Do you have any idea? → <u>Hai qualche idea?</u>**

1.   Do you have any fruit? _____

2.   Do you have any sweaters? _____

3.   I don't have any shirts. _____

4.   Did you buy a blouse? _____

5.   No, I didn't buy any blouses. _____

6.   Are there some boys in the pool? _____

7.   No, there aren't any boys in the pool. _____

8.   Do you have any cats at home? _____

9.   No, I don't have any cats at home _____

10.   Do you have any suitcases in the car? _____

11.   No, I don't have any suitcases in the car. _____

D. Answer these questions, first affirmatively, and then, negatively. **Example: C'è qualcosa in frigorifero? → <u>Sì, c'è. No, non c'è niente.</u>**

1.   C'è qualcosa nel forno? _____

2.   C'è qualcosa nella valigia? _____

3.   C'è qualcosa sul tavolo? _____

Yes, sir; no, sir

4.   C'è qualcosa in camera da letto? _____

5.   C'è qualcosa nel portafoglio? (*wallet*)? _____

6.   C'è qualcosa nell'auto? _____.

E. Answer these questions, first affirmatively, and then, negatively. **Example: C'è qualcuno in biblioteca?** → **Sì, c'è qualcuno. No, non c'è nessuno.**

1.   C'è qualcuno nel giardino? _____

2.   C'è qualcuno in casa? _____

3.   C'è qualcuno nella pescheria? _____

4.   C'è qualcuno nell'ufficio? _____

5.   C'è qualcuno per strada? _____

6.   C'è qualcuno nell'edificio? _____

F. Answer these questions, first affirmatively, then, negatively. **Example: Ci sono quadri (paintings) nel museo?** → **Sì, ce ne sono alcuni. No, non ce ne sono.** Remember: **Nessun, nessuno, and nessuna** do not have a plural form.

1.   Ci sono fiori nel giardino? _____

2.   Ci sono bambini nel collegio? _____

3.   Ci sono libri nella biblioteca? _____

4.   Ci sono persone alla festa? _____

5.   Ci sono sedie nella classe? _____

6.   Ci sono cani nel parco? _____

G. Express these sentences using double negatives. **Example: C'è qualcosa di interessante al cinema →**
Non c'è niente di interessante al cinema.

1. C'è qualcosa di buono in cucina: _____

2. Ho qualche fiore nel mio giardino: _____

3. Sofía studia sempre la lezione: _____

4. Mettono qualcosa nell'auto: _____

5. Ricevono sempre i loro amici: _____

6. Vendono anche le banane in quel fruttivendolo: _____

H. Choose among these indefinite pronouns to complete the sentences: **niente – nessuno - nessuno -
nessuna** or these negative adverbs: **mai - né - neanche - mai**

1. _____ c'è _____ nel frigorifero.

2. Maria e Daniele _____ discutono.

3. Non mi piace _____ la carne _____ il pollo.

4. Non mi piace _____ quel giovane.

5. _____ sa il suo nome.

6. Non voglio andare al ristorante. Io _____ voglio andare.

7. Non c'è _____ hotel in questa città.

8. _____ fiore è bello come questo.

I. Answer the following questions with a negative response. Try to use a double negative.

Remember: **nessun, nessuno and nessuna** do not have a plural form.

1. Condividete qualcosa? No, _____

2. Tomás riceve qualcosa per il suo compleanno (*for his birthday*)? No, _____
    _____

3.   C'è qualche ristorante in questa (*this*) via? No, _____

4.   Canti mai? No, _____

5.   Hanno fatto qualche lavoro per domani (*in the morning*)? No, _____

      _____

6.   Leggete qualche giornale la domenica? No, _____

7.   C'è qualche fiore in inverno? No, _____

8.   Vai sempre al supermercato il sabato? No, _____

9.   I turisti visitano qualche parco? No, _____

10.   Voi mangiate carne? No, _____

J. Turn these sentences into negative ones. In some cases, it will be a double negative. **Example: Sai qualcosa di francese? No, non so niente di francese.**

Remember: **Nessun, nessuno and nessuna** do not have a plural form.

1.   Sta sempre giù di morale. _____

2.   Noi facciamo un po' di sport oggi. _____

3.   Anche Maria deve comprare dei libri. _____

4.   Questo supermercato è un po' piccolo. _____

5.   Qualcuno studia in biblioteca. _____

6.   Tante bambine ballano al collegio. _____

7.   Ci sono fruttivendoli qui (*here*)? No, _____

8.   Martino beve acqua. _____

9.   Voi pulite sempre la casa. _____

10.   Conosco tutti i suoi amici. _____

ANSWER KEY

Practice. 1.1

A. 1. No, Teresa non vuole mangiare niente. 2. No, Teresa non vuole bere niente. 3. No, Teresa non vuole niente. 4. No, Teresa non mangia mai la sera.

B. 1. niente 2. nessuno 3. nessuno 4. mai 5. neanche 6. qualche 7. qualcuno 8. alcuno 9. sempre 10. anche

C. 1. Hai della frutta? 2. Hai un maglione? 3. Non ho nessuna camicia. 4. Hai comprato una casacca? 5. No, non ho comprato nessuna casacca. 6. Ci sono bambini in piscina? 7. No, non c'è nessun bambino in piscina. 8. Hai dei gatti in casa? 9. No, non ho nessun gatto in casa. 10. Hai qualche valigia nell'auto? 11. No, non ho nessuna valigia nell'auto.

D. 1. Sì, Ho qualcosa. No, non c'è niente. 2. Sì, c'è qualcosa. Non c'è niente. 3. Sì, c'è qualcosa. No, non c'è niente. 4. Sì, c'è qualcosa. No, non c'è niente. 5. Sì, c'è qualcosa. No, non c'è niente. 6. Sì, c'è qualcosa. No, non c'è niente.

E. 1. Sì, c'è qualcuno. No, non c'è nessuno. 2. Sì, c'è qualcuno. No, non c'è nessuno. 3. Sì, c'è qualcuno. No, non c'è nessuno. 4. Sì, c'è qualcuno. No, non c'è nessuno.5. Sì, c'è qualcuno. No, non c'è nessuno. 6. Sì, c'è qualcuno. No, non c'è nessuno.

F. 1. Sì, ce ne sono alcune. No, non ce n'è nessuna. 2. Sì, ce ne sono alcuni. No, non ce n'è nessuno. 3. Sì, ce ne sono alcuni. No, non ce n'è nessuno. 4. Sì, ce ne sono alcune. No, non ce n'è nessuna. 5. Sì, ce ne sono alcune. No, non ce n'è nessuna. 6. Sì, ce ne sono alcuni. No, non ce n'è nessuno.

G. 1. Non c'è niente di buono in cucina. 2. Non ho nessun fiore nel mio giardino. 3. Neanche Maria studia lì. 4. Sofia non studia mai la lezione. 5. Non mettono niente nell'auto 6. Non ricevono mai i loro amici. 7. Non vendono neanche banane in quel fruttivendolo.

H.   1. mai... niente 3. mai 3. né... né 4. niente 5. nessuno 6. neanche 7. nessun 8. nessuna

I.   1. No, non condividiamo niente. 2. No, Tommaso non riceve niente per il suo compleanno. 3. No, non c'è nessun ristorante in questa via. 4. No, non canto mai. 5. No, non hanno fatto nessun lavoro per domani. 6. No, non leggono nessun giornale la domenica. 7. No, non c'è nessun fiore in inverno. 8. No, non vado mai al supermercato il sabato. 9. No, i turisti non visitano mai nessun parco. 10. No, voi non mangiate carne.

J.   1. Non sta giù di morale. 2. Noi non facciamo nessuno sport oggi. 3. Neanche Maria deve comprare dei libri. 4. Questo supermercato non è affatto piccolo. 5. Nessuno studia in biblioteca. 6. Nessuna bambina balla al collegio. 7. No, non c'è nessun fruttivendolo qui. 8. No, Martino non beve niente. 9. Voi non pulite mai la casa (or Voi non pulite mai niente). 10. Non conosco nessuno dei suoi amici (or Non conosco nessun amico di lui).

LESSON 12

YOU, AND YOU, AND YOU

CONJUNCTIONS AND INDEFINITE ADJECTIVES

1 CONJUNCTIONS

Don't be intimidated by that big word! Conjunctions are some of the most common components of everyday language. They connect other words, phrases, and clauses. For example, in that last sentence 'and' was the conjunction, because it unites the rest of the sentence.

Some other examples of conjunctions are 'or' and 'but.' They allow us to say things like 'She came by, but she didn't come in.'

By learning conjunctions in Italian, you'll be able to construct slightly more complex sentences. Although they aren't hard to construct, they can convey a whole new layer of meaning.

In Italian, there are two types of conjunctions:

- ➲   Coordinating conjunctions ('but,' 'and,' 'or')

- ➲   Subordinating conjunctions ('because,' 'although')

What's the difference?

Coordinating conjunctions join two parts of a sentence that are equal in importance, e.g., 'Tina loves Instagram <u>and</u> Bob loves Facebook.' You know they're equal because if you removed the conjunction, you would still understand that Tina loves Instagram and Bob loves Facebook.

Subordinating conjunctions, on the other hand, connect parts of a sentence that don't convey the same message when they're independent. E.g., 'Tina loves Instagram <u>because</u> she's a fan of photography.' If you removed the conjunction in this sentence, you wouldn't understand that the reason Tina loves Instagram is because she's a fan of photography.

These same differences apply to coordinating and subordinating conjunctions in Italian. Understanding their purpose will help you navigate them.

COORDINATING CONJUNCTIONS

Combine Elements Together (Copulative Conjunctions)	e	and	Mangia **e** beve (*he eats and drinks*).
	né	nor	Non mangio **né** pane **né** gallette (*He doesn't eat bread nor crackers*).
Show an Opposition or Difference (Adversative Conjunctions)	**però**/ma	but	È intelligente **ma** svogliato (*He's intelligent but lazy*).
	ma	but	Ha un lavoro **ma** non è felice (*She has a job but isn't happy*).
	Tuttavia (usually used after a semi-colon)	however, nevertheless, but	Ha molto denaro; **tuttavia**, non lo condivide (*She has a lot of money but doesn't share it*).
	anche se/sebbene	even if, though, although	Il film è bello, **anche se** lungo (*The movie is good, even if it's long*).
	ma/bensì	but	Non mangio carne **ma** pesce.
Show Options (Disjunctive Conjunctions)	**o**	or	Maria ritorna a mezzogiorno **o** alle 13:00 (*María comes back at 12:00 p.m. or at 1:00 p.m.*).
	o	or (used when the word following the disjunctive conjunction "o" begins with the vowel "o" or the silent letter "h" followed by the vowel "o")	Laura organizza **o** sistema i documenti (*Laura organizes or arranges the papers*).

You, and you, and you

Show Alternation (Distributive Conjunctions)	**o... o**	*either... or*	**O** studi **o** non guardi la TV (*either you study, or you don't watch TV*).
	sia... che	*either... or*	Studiano **sia** al parco, **che** in biblioteca (*either they study in the park or in the library*).
	tanto... quanto	*both*	**Tanto Pietro quanto** Maria sono bravi studenti (*both Pedro and María are good students*).
	sia... sia	*whether... or*	Il matrimonio è condividere la vita **sia** nelle gioie **sia** nei dolori (*Marriage is sharing life whether in happiness or in sorrow*).

1.2. Practice

A. Find the right conjunctions: e - o. If the sentence is not translated, go ahead, and translate it.

1. María and Inés: _____

2. There are ten or eleven children: _____

3. Get the key and try to open the door: Prendi la chiave _____ prova ad aprire la porta.

4. He calls and invites us: _____

5. She saw something or heard a noise: Vide qualcosa _____ udì un rumore.

6. She knows how to read and write very well. _____

B. Fill in the blanks with the conjunctions **e, o**, or **ma**

1. Il bambino mangia una banana _____ una mela.

2. Martino lavora _____ studia?

3. Cerco il mio cane _____ non lo trovo.

4. Lo ripeto due _____ tre volte (*times*).

5. Avete cantato _____ ballato tutta la notte.

6. Sono francese _____ vivo in Italia.

7. Vieni alle otto _____ alle nove del mattino.

8. Luisa lavora tanto _____ guadagna (*earns*) poco (little).

C. Let's practice adversative conjunctions: **però, ma, tuttavia, anche se, bensì.** Fill in the blanks with the right conjunction:

1. Mangio poco _____ sono grasso.

2. Non lavora oggi in ufficio _____ domani.

3. Tommaso sa tante cose _____ è una persona umile (*humble*).

4. Ha l'auto; _____ gli piace camminare.

5. Viaggia tanto, _____ non ha tanto denaro.

6. _____ non ricevo il giornale, lo leggo tutti i giorni.

D. Circle the right conjunction in each sentence.

1. Cammino tutti i giorni _____ fa bene alla salute.

    perché - tuttavia

2. Essi mangiano al ristorante tutti i giorni _____ esse mangiano casa.

    ma - né

3. Teresa impara il tedesco _____ non ne ha bisogno.

LEARN ITALIAN
GRAMMAR WORKBOOK

né – anche se

4. _____ Elena _____ Cristiano bevono vino.

anche se - né

5. Elena _____ Ilario sono avvocati.

e - né

6. _____ Pietro _____ Sofia sono francesi.

anche se - tanto   quanto - né

7. Compriamo _____ vendiamo roba usata (*used clothes*).

e - ma

8. Andiamo al ristorante _____ non c'è da mangiare a casa.

perché - ma

9. Studia tanto; _____ non impara tanto.

anche se - tuttavia

2 SUBORDINATING CONJUNCTIONS

As we mentioned earlier, subordinating conjunctions connect parts of a sentence that are dependent on each other.

SUBORDINATING CONJUNCTIONS

Showing Cause (Cause Conjunctions)	**perché**	*because*	È stanca **perché** lavora tanto (*She's tired because she works a lot*).
	poiché/dato che/ visto che	*since, as, because*	Sto a casa **visto che** piove (*I'm home because it's raining*).
	siccome	*since, as, because*	**Siccome è occupato, non ha tempo** (*Since he's busy, he doesn't have any time*).
Elaborating (Relative Conjunctions)	**che**	*that*	Mi ha detto **che** sono il suo migliore amico (*He told me that I was his best friend*).
Making Comparisons (Comparative Conjunctions)	**così come**	*just as*	José è alto, **così come** sua sorella (*José is tall, just as his sister*).
	e anche	*so to*	Sa il francese, **e anche** il tedesco (*He knows French, so too German*).
	tanto quanto	*as*	Maria è simpatica **tanto quanto** Clara (*Maria is as nice as Clara*).
To Show an Obstacle Doesn't Prevent Action (Concessive Conjunctions)	**ebbene**	*although, even though, though*	La biblioteca è chiusa, **anche se è mezzogiorno** (*The library is closed, even though it's 12:00 p.m.*).
	nonostante	*even though, despite the fact that*	È triste, **nonostante** abbia tanti amici (*He's sad, despite the fact that he has lots of friends*).

You, and you, and you

To Show Conditions (Conditional Conjunctions)	**se**	*if*	Pago con carta di credito **se** devo (*I pay with a credit card if I need to*).
	a meno che	*unless*	Corro tutti i giorni **a meno che** non piove (*I run every day unless it rains*).
To Give a Sense of Time and Order (Time Conjunctions)	**mentre**	*while, meanwhile*	Cammina **mentre** parla al telefono (*She walks while she talks on the phone*).

Common Mistakes:

The conjunction **che** is essential in Italiano, even though it is often not translated in English. **Che** as a conjunction which means *that*.

Credo che lei sia felice (*I believe that she is happy*)

Note that in English, you can say, *I believe she is happy* (without the "that"). Be careful! You can also say **Credo sia felice** in Italian, omitting the **che**. But in some cases, specifically when there is the subject, you need to use the **che**.

Credo la bambina sia felice X

Credo che la bambina sia felice ✓

2.1. Practice

A. Let's practice the relative conjunction **si**. Join these sentences. **Example: Maria / non/ sapere/ se / Juan / avere bisogno / qualcosa: <u>Maria non sa se Juan ha bisogno di qualcosa.</u>**

1. Pietro e Luigi/ non / sapere / se / suoi amici / ritornare:

    _____

2. Mirta / domanda (*ask*) / se / c'è / esame / domani:

    _____

3. José / decidere / se / salire / sul monte Fitz Roy:

    _____

4. Voi / non / sapere / se / Paula / ha bisogno / qualcosa / per la festa:

    _____

5. Lei / domandare / se / gli impiegati / lavorare / bene:

    _____

6. Tu / decidere / se / bere / caffè / o / tè:

    _____

B. Let's practice the relative conjunction **che**. Remember? The one you should never omit in Italian. Join these sentences. **Example: Abbiamo una festa. Mi dice. → Mi dice che abbiamo una festa.**

1. Abitiamo in via Oro. Lei sa: _____

2. Viaggiamo tutto l'anno. Juan pensa: _____

3. Il signor Ortiz ripara forni. Io credo: _____

4. A José piace mangiare. Dice Giovanna: _____

5. È tardi. La professoressa ci dice: _____

6. I bambini hanno bisogno di matite nuove. La madre dice: _____

C. Join both sentences with a subordinate conjunction: **perché - ma - anche se - che**. Example: È un buon professore. Io credo → <u>**Io credo che sia un buon professore.**</u>

1. Mi piace. I miei figli ordinano da soli.

2. Lavoro tanto. Guadagno poco.

3. Fa freddo. C'è il sole.

4. Sta soffiando troppo vento per correre. Martino crede.

5. I pomodori sono verdi. Mi spiega il fruttivendolo.

6. Arrivi presto. Esci presto.

3 INDEFINITE ADJECTIVES

An indefinite adjective is an adjective used to describe a noun in a non-specific way. It agrees with the noun in number and sometimes gender. Many indefinite adjectives in Italian are identical to Italian indefinite pronouns.

Examples of indefinite adjectives are:

C'è **qualche** mela (*There are a few apples*).

C'è **qualche** possibilità (*possibility*) di viaggiare (*travel*).

C'è **tanto** sole.

È la **stessa** casa.

Mi serve **qualche** vestito.

Il professore **tutti** gli esercizi.

SINGULAR		PLURAL		
masculine	feminine	masculine	feminine	
alcun	alcuna	alcuni	alcune	*some, a few*
nessun	nessuna	-	-	*none, neither*
ogni	ogni	-	-	*each*
certo	certa	certi	certe	*certain*
stesso	stessa	stessi	stesse	*same*
tanto	tanta	tanti	tante	*many, much, a lot*
altro	altra	altri	altre	*other*
poco	poca	pochi	poche	*few, a little*
alcune	-	alcuni	-	*some, any*
tanto	tanta	tanti	tante	*so many, so much*
tutto	tutta	tutti	tutte	*all*
-	-	vari	varie	*several, some*

── Common Mistake: ──

Indefinite adjectives are used in place of an article, **not with one**.

Don't say **Ci sono le alcune mele** X

Say, instead, **Si sono alcune mele** ✓

3.1.   Practice

A. Complete the sentences with the right indefinite adjective. **Example: Paolo compra solo _____ mela →**
Paolo compra solo qualche mela.

1.   _____ persone lavorano solo in casa propria.

2.   Ci sono _____ uccelli che sembrano(*looks like*) una giungla (*jungle*)

3.   È il _____ cappello che ha Juan.

4.   Susanna ha _____ casa sulla spiaggia.

5.   _____ persone condividono l'appartamento con gli amici.

6.   _____ giorno che passa è peggio (*is worse*).

7.   Quel cantante ha composto (*composed*) _____ canzoni simili (*similar*).

8.   Piove _____ la settimana.

B. Translate the following sentences with conjunctions and indefinite adjectives:

1.   Lei ha tanti cani e gatti.

      _____

2.   Maria ha diverse figlie, ma non ha figli.

      _____

3.   Sia Luigi che Juan hanno pochi amici.

      _____

4.   Non legge né riviste (*magazines*) né quotidiani (*newspapers*).

      _____

5.   Conosce altri paesi perché viaggia tanto.

      _____

6.   Ha la stessa auto di Laura.

      _____

7.   Conosce ogni strada di Parigi, ma non conosce la propria città (*her own city*).

    _____

8.   Parla alcune lingue, ma non parla inglese.

    _____

9.   È la stessa amicizia, anche se siamo più vecchi.

    _____

10.   Tutte le lingue sono utili (*useful*), ma alcune sono più utili (*useful*) di altre.

    _____

C. Elena has a positive outlook on life. Roberto has a negative outlook on life. Change Elena's statements to the opposite to know what Robert thinks. **Example: Ho pochi problemi → Ho tanti problemi.**

1.   Tutti i giorni sono belli → _____

2.   Ho pochi dolori → _____

3.   Ci sono tante cose belle nella vita → _____

4.   Ho tanti amici → _____

5.   Certi giorni sono brutti → _____

6.   Nessun compito (*task*) è impossibile → _____

ANSWER KEY

Practice. 1.1

A.   1. Maria e Ines 2. Ci sono dieci o undici bambini 3. Prendi la chiave e cerca di aprire la porta 4. Lui ci chiama e ci invita. 5. Ho visto qualcosa e ho sentito un rumore. 6. Sa leggere e scrivere molto bene.

B.   1. e 2. o 3. ma 4. o 5. e 6. ma 7. o 8. ma

C.   1. ma 2. bensì 3. ma 4. tuttavia 5. anche se 6. anche se

D.   1. perché 2. ma 3. anche se 4. Né... né 5. e 6. Tanto... quanto 7. e 8. perché 9. tuttavia

Practice. 2.1

A.   1. Pietro e Luigi non sanno se i loro amici ritornano. 2. Mirta domanda se c'è un esame domani. 3. José decide se salire sul monte Fitz Roy. 4. Voi non sapete se Paola ha bisogno di qualcosa per la festa. 5. Lei domanda se gli impiegati lavorano bene. 6. Tu decidi se bevi caffè o tè.

B.   1. Lei sa che abitiamo in via Oro. 2. Juan pensa che viaggiamo tutto l'anno. 3. Io credo che il signor Ortiz ripari forni. 4. Giovanna dice che a José piace mangiare. 5. La professoressa ci dice che è tardi. 6. La madre dice che i bambini hanno bisogno di matite nuove.

C.   1. Me piace che i miei figli ordinino da soli. 2. Lavoro molto ma guadagno poco. 3. Anche se fa freddo, c'è il sole. 4. Martino crede che stia soffiando troppo vento per correre. 5. Il fruttivendolo mi spiega che i pomodori sono verdi. 6. Arrivi presto perché esci presto.

Practice. 3.1

A.   1. tante 2. molti 3. stesso 4. altra 5. alcune 6. ogni 7. altre 8. tutta

B.   1. She has many dogs and cats. 2. Maria has several daughters, but she has no sons. 3. Both Luis and Juan have few friends. 4. She/he doesn't read magazines or newspapers. 5. She/he knows other countries since she/he travels a lot. 6. She/he has the same car as Laura. 7. She/he knows every street in Paris, but she/he doesn't know her/his own city. 8. She/he speaks some languages, but she/he doesn't speak English. 9. It's the same friendship, though we're older. 10. All languages are useful, even if some are more useful than others.

C.   1. Nessun giorno è bello 2. Ho tanti dolori 3. Ci sono così poche cose belle nella vita 4. Ho pochi amici 5. Tutti i giorni sono brutti. 6. Ogni compito è impossibile.

LESSON 13

I LIKE APPLES

LIKES AND DISLIKES

It would be impossible to get to know other people and allow them to get to know you without learning to express likes and dislikes. They convey our opinions and other key parts of our personality. By using **mi piace** and **non mi piace**, we can finally tell people what we really think!

1 CONSTRUCTIONS WITH MI PIACE AND NON MI PIACE

Poema XV
Pablo Neruda

Mi piace quando taci

Perché sei come assente,

E mi ascolti da lontano,

E la mia voce non ti tocca. [...]

"I like it when you're silent / because you're sort of absent / and you hear me from afar / and my voice doesn't touch you."

This is part of a poem by Chilean poet Pablo Neruda (1904-1973), who wrote in various styles, including passionate love poems, and won the Nobel Prize in Literature in 1971.

The verb **piacere** is used in Italian to express likes and dislikes:

- ⮌ **Mi piace leggere** (*I like to read*)
- ⮌ **Non mi piacciono i gatti** (*I don't like cats*)

But **piacere** does not literally mean *to like*.

Strictly speaking, *piacere* means *to be pleasing (to someone).* It needs to be used with an indirect object to make complete sense. This indirect object is whatever it is you're expressing your affection or fondness for.

The indirect object can be a pronoun (mi, ti, gli, ci, vi, gli) or a person/object/animal preceded by a → <u>a + person/name/object.</u>

For example:

A Maria piace il gelato (*Maria likes ice-cream*)

A me piacciono (mi piacciono) i cavalli (*I like horses*)

A Juan e Cristina piace la musica classica (*Juan and Cristina like classical music*).

A sentence like, **A Martino piace mangiare** has two indirect objects: **gli** and **a Martino. A Martino** is used to add emphasis or to clarify who or what the indirect object pronoun is (**gli** could be a woman, an animal, or almost anything).

I like apples

Notice, too, that the verb **piacere** must agree with its subject, i.e., the person or thing that is liked, *not* the person who is being described. In the sentences above, we used both **piace** and **piacciono** to agree with the different nouns.

A Martino piacciono i cavalli → **piacciono** matches **cavalli**, not Martín.

To say that you *don't* like something, you need to add **no** before the indirect object pronoun.

Non mi piacciono i cani (*I don't like dogs*)

A loro non piacciono i gatti (*they don't like cats*)

Ci piacciono le moto (*we don't like motorcycles*)

Indirect Object Pronouns

mi: to, for me

ti: to, for you

gli: to, for you, him, her, it

ci: to, for us

vi: to, for you

gli/a loro: to, for you, them

Now check these sentences:

➲ **A Martino piacciono le mappe**: *Martin likes maps* (*or Maps are pleasing to Martin*). In this case, since maps is plural, "piacciono" is in the plural form. **Gli** is the indirect object and **A Martino** is used in addition to the indirect object pronoun for clarification or emphasis.

➲ **A me piace (mi piace) lo sport**: *I like sports* (*or Sports are pleasing to me*). Again, **sport** agrees with the singular **piace**. **Mi** is the indirect object pronoun and **A me** is used as emphasis.

➲ **Le piacciono i fiori?:** *Do you like flowers?* (*Are flowers pleasing to you?*). **I fiori** agrees with the plural **piacciono**. **Le** is the indirect object. **A Lei (*formal*)** is used for clarification (since **le** can also refer to someone else).

➲ **A loro piace (gli piace) il teatro**: *They like the theatre* (*The theatre is pleasing to them*). **Il teatro** is singular and agrees with **piace.** The indirect object is **gli** and **A loro** is used for emphasis.

TIP

Just as in English, you can combine **piacere + a verb** (*I like running*). In Italian, **piacere** is combined with the **infinitive** of the verb (not the gerund, like in English): **gustar + verbo all'infinito.**

Example: **Ti piace correre** (*you like running*), **mi piace guardare la TV** (*I like watching TV*), **a loro piace cucinare** (*they like cooking*).

Do not say: Mi piace correndo X

Say: Mi piace correre ✔

Speak Abroad
Academy

Vocabulary: food

Something that we all have strong opinions about is food! It's time to expand your vocabulary and get to know the different Italian words for food. Using what we just learned, can you express which types of food below you like or dislike?

carne	[kahr-neh]	*meat*
pollo	[poh-yoh]	*chicken*
pesce	[peh-scheh]	*fish*
hamburger	[ahm-boor-gehr]	*hamburgers*
pomodoro	[poh-moh-doh-roh]	*tomato*
lattuga	[laht-too-gah]	*lettuce*
mela	[meh-lah]	*apple*
arancia	[ah-rahn-chee-ah]	*orange*
patate	[pah-tah-teh]	*potatoes*
banana	[bah-nah-nah]	*banana*
cipolla	[chee-pohl-lah]	*onion*
pane	[pah-neh]	*bread*
latte	[laht-teh]	*milk*
acqua	[ah-kwah]	*water*

I like apples

caffè	[kahf-feh]	*coffee*
tè	[teh]	*tea*
zucchero	[tsook-keh-roh]	*sugar*
caramelle	[kah-rah-mehl-leh]	*candy*

1.1.   Practice

A. Write an indirect object pronoun for each subject pronoun.

1.   A noi _____ piace.

2.   A voi _____ piace.

3.   A Lei _____ piace.

4.   A loro _____ piace.

5.   A Juan e Matías _____ piace.

6.   A me _____ piace.

7.   A te _____ piace.

8.   A Juan _____ piace.

9.   A Elena _____ piace.

B. Translate the following with the two indirect objects. **Example: She likes candy → A lei piacciono le caramelle.**

1.   I like the car _____

2.   They like onions _____

3.   We don't like reading _____

4.   You (sing.) like bananas _____

5.   You (fam.pl) like working _____

6.   Marcos likes studying _____

7.   Elsa likes tomatoes _____

8.   My father likes to eat _____

9.   My mother likes fish _____

10.   The boys don't like milk _____

11.   Maria likes chicken _____

C. Join the words to make a sentence. Make sure you include two indirect objects (the pronoun + whoever the action is for). **Example: non / piacciono /le / banane / a Mirta: <u>A Mirta non piacciono le banane.</u>**

1.   correre / a noi / piace: _____

2.   no / piacciono / le verdure / ai bambini _____

3.   quelle scarpe / piacciono / me _____

4.   le feste / a Luigi e Teresa / piacciono _____

5.   suonare il piano / a Elena / piace _____

6.   piace / mi / il pesce _____

D. Pick one of the items below and say you like it. Pick the other one to say you don't like it. You can switch the items according to what you like. You may use an adversative conjunction (**ma, anche se, tuttavia)** or a copulative conjunction (**e**).

Example: **mangiare carne? Mangiare pesce? <u>Non mi piace mangiare carne, ma mi piace mangiare pesce.</u>**

1.   Leo Messi? Cristiano Ronaldo? _____

2.   mangiare hamburger? mangiare pasta? _____

3.   il caffè? il tè? _____

4.   l'attrice Meryl Streep? l'attrice Judy Dench? _____

5.   il tennista Medvedev? il tennista Federer? _____

6.   studiare in biblioteca? studiare in sala da pranzo? _____

7.   i cani? i gatti? _____

8.   viaggiare in treno? viaggiare in auto? _____

I like apples

E. Complete the sentences by conjugating **piacere** according to its subject and adding the right pronoun (le/les). **Example: A Isabella _____ i bambini → A Isabella piacciono i bambini.**

1. A Sebastiano e Nicola _____ lo sport.

2. A voi _____ gli orologi costosi.

3. A te _____ le moto.

4. A noi _____ imparare l'italiano.

5. A me _____ i cioccolatini.

6. A Lei _____ le automobili.

F. Complete these questions making **piacere** concur with the subject and adding the appropriate personal pronoun. **Example: (lui / piacere) _____ il teatro? → A lui piace il teatro?**

1. (noi / piacere) _____ le feste?

2. (Teresa / piacere) _____ la sua università?

3. (loro / piacere) _____ ricevere gente in casa?

4. (io / piacere) _____ fare yoga?

5. (tu / piacere) _____ il pesce?

6. (Lei / piacere) _____ viaggiare?

G. Complete with a + pronoun + pronoun + verb **piacere. Example _____ (io) studiare lingue→ A me piace studiare lingue.**

1. _____ (noi) lavorare.

2. _____ (voi) vivere da soli.

3. _____ (voi) camminare nel parco il sabato.

4. _____ (Carolina e Luigi) salire sui monti.

5. _____ (tu) invitare gli amici a casa tua.

6. _____ (loro) viaggiare per il mondo.

H. Rewrite these sentences by correcting the mistakes:

7. A me ci piace le caramelle: _____
8. A te ti piace il pane: _____
9. A voi mi piace il latte: _____
10. A te mi piace il caffè _____
11. A loro ci piacciono le arance: _____
12. A lui ti piace la carne: _____

Vocabulary: members of the family

padre	[pah-dreh]	father
madre	[mah-dreh]	mother
figlia	[fee-lyah]	daughter
figlio	[fee-lyoh]	son
nonno	[nohn-noh]	grandfather
nonna	[nohn-nah]	grandmother
zio/zia	[tsyoh/tsyah]	uncle/aunt
cugino/a	[koo-jee-noh/koo-jee-nah]	cousin
nipote	[nee-poh-teh]	nephew/niece

I like apples

I. Dove andiamo in vacanza? (*where do we go on vacations?*)

The Pérez family each have their own idea of a good vacation and where they prefer to go. Turn the suggested separate elements into a sentence. Remember to include the indirect object that clarifies or adds emphasis. **Example: padre / nuotare Al padre piace nuotare.**

1.   nonno / cucinare

    _____

2.   fratello / fare surf (*to do surf*)

    _____

3.   zia / leggere libri

    _____

4.   cugini / comprare vestiti (*go shopping for clothes*)

    _____

5.   padre / mangiare e bere

    _____

6.   figlia / cercare telline sulla riva (*look for seashells on the shore*)

    _____

7.   madre / la tranquillità

    _____

8.   nipoti / correre sulla spiaggia (*run on the beach*)

    _____

2 EXPRESSING WANTS IN A DIRECT AND POLITE WAY

You've learned how to express your like and dislike for something, but what about your wants? How can you tell someone that you want something?

In Italian, you use the verb **volere** to express **wants**, e.g., **Voglio un caffè** (*I want a coffee*)

How do you say you don't want something? For this, we'll use **non** again.

To say you don't want something, just add a **non** before the verb: **Non voglio un caffè** (*I don't want a coffee*)

As with **piacere,** you can also add an infinitive to **volere/desiderare** when you *want to do something*, e.g., **Voglio imparare il tedesco** (*I want to learn German*).

Sometimes it's not polite to ask directly for something. For example, if you're asking for a map in a hotel lobby, it's more polite to say, **Vorrei una mappa** (*I would like a map*) than **Voglio una mappa** (*I want a map*).

When you want to express what you would like or wouldn't like, in Italian you say, **Vorrei / Non vorrei**.

Of course, **vorrei** is also used when you're wishing or pining for something: **Mi piacerebbe conoscere Luigi** (*I would like to meet Luis*). In other words, it's a way of expressing your wants in a less direct way, which is essential for politeness.

With **vorrei** you can also add an infinitive for something you *would like to do*: **Mi piacerebbe scalare l'Everest**.

2.1.   Practice

A. Choose what you would say in each scenario, depending on whether you can be more direct or need to be more polite:

1.   You're at a bar and ask the waiter for a glass of water: _____ (voglio / vorrei) un bicchier d'acqua.

2.   You're expressing your need for sleep to a friend _____ (voglio / vorrei) dormire.

3.   You're explaining to a professor that you would like to speak Italian well. _____(vorrei / voglio) parlare bene l'italiano.

4.   You're asking a salesperson at a store to hand you that green dress: _____ (voglio / vorrei) quel vestito verde.

5.   You're telling your friend you want to fix the roof. _____ (voglio / vorrei) riparare il tetto.

ANSWER KEY

Practice. 1.1

A.   1. ci 2. vi 3. gli 4. gli 5. a loro 6. mi 7. ti 8. le 9. le

B.   1. A me piace l'auto. 2. A loro piacciono le cipolle. 3. A noi non piace leggere. 4. A te piacciono le banane 5. A voi piace lavorare. 6. A Marcos piace studiare. 7. A Elsa piacciono i pomodori. 8. A mio padre piace mangiare. 9. A mia madre piace il pesce. 10. Ai bambini non piace il latte. 11. A Maria piace il pollo.

C.   1. Ci piace correre. 2. Ai bambini non piacciono le verdure. 3. Mi piacciono quelle scarpe. 4. A Luigi e Teresa piacciono le feste. 5. A Elena piace suonare il piano. 6. A me piace il pesce.

D. (Answers may vary) 1. Non mi piace Cristiano Ronaldo, ma mi piace Leo Messi. 2. Non mi piace mangiare pasta, ma mi piace mangiare hamburger. 3. Non mi piace il caffè; tuttavia, mi piace il tè. 4. Non mi piace l'attrice (*actress*) Judy Dench, ma mi piace l'attrice Meryl Streep. 5. Non mi piace il tennista Medvedev, però mi piace il tennista Federer. 6. Non mi piace studiare in sala da pranzo, ma mi piace studiare in biblioteca. 7. Non mi piacciono i gatti, però mi piacciono i cani. 8. Non mi piace viaggiare in treno; tuttavia, mi piace viaggiare in auto.

E. 1. a loro piacciono 2. vi piacciono 3. ti piacciono 4. ci piace 5. mi piace 6. le piacciono

F. 1. A noi piacciono le feste? 2. A Teresa piace la sua università? 3. A loro piace ricevere gente in casa? 4. A me piace fare yoga? 5. A te piace il pesce? 6. A Lei piace viaggiare?

G. 1. A noi piace lavorare. 2. A voi piace vivere da soli. 3. A voi piace camminare nel parco il sabato. 4. A Carolina e Luigi piace scalare le montagne. 5. Ti piace invitare amici in casa tua. 6. A loro piace viaggiare per il mondo.

H. 1. A me piacciono le caramelle. 2. A te piace il pane. 3. A voi piace il latte. 4. A te piace il caffè. 5. A loro piacciono le arance. 6. A lui piace la carne.

I. 1. Al nonno piace cucinare. 2. Al fratello piace fare surf. 3. Alla zia piace leggere libri. 4. Ai cugini piace comprare vestiti. 5. Al padre piace mangiare e bere. 6. Alla figlia piace cercare conchiglie sulla riva. 7. Alla madre piace la tranquillità. 8. Ai nipoti piace correre sulla spiaggia.

Practice. 2.1

A. 1. Vorrei un bicchiere d'acqua. 2. Voglio dormire. 3. Vorrei parlare bene lo spagnolo. 4. Vorrei quel vestito verde. 5. Voglio riparare il tetto.

I like apples

LESSON 14

PREPOSITIONS I

THE HAT IS ON THE CHAIR

1 INTRODUCTION TO PREPOSITIONS

Again, don't be afraid of the big word. We use prepositions all the time and they're not complex. They're words like 'on,' 'over,' or 'until,' which are important for describing space and time.

If you're trying to help someone, find something, prepositions allow you to describe to them which part of the room they would find the object in. Is it *under* the bed? *On* the table? *In* the laundry hamper?

It also describes time. If you're trying to organize plans with your friends, prepositions would help you arrange an appropriate time. Can you only hang out *at* 8 PM? *After* work? *Before* your favourite TV show starts playing. Or maybe just *until* you start feeling drunk?

The good news is that, unlike most words in Italian, prepositions in Italian don't change! They have no number or gender, and always remain the same. Phew!

Here is the list of simple prepositions:

a	[ah]	*at, to*
prima	[pree-mah]	*before*
sotto	[soht-toh]	*under*
con	[kohn]	*with*
contra	[kohn-troh]	*against*
di	[deeh]	*of, from*
da	[dah]	*after, since, from*
durante	[doo-rahn-teh]	*during*
in	[eehn]	*in, on*
tra/fra	[trah frah]	*among, between*
verso	[vehr-soh]	*toward*
fino a	[fee-noh ah]	*until, up to, as far as*
eccetto	[eh-tchet-toh]	*except*
per	[pehr]	*for, in order to*
da	[dah]	*by, for*
tranne	[trahn-neh]	*except, save*

secondo	[seh-kohn-doh]	*according to*
senza	[sehn-tsah]	*without*
sopra	[soh-prah]	*on, upon, over, above*
dietro	[dee-eh-troh]	*after, behind*

Most Common Prepositions: in - di - con

Let's start practicing the three most common prepositions in Italian. We will start with these three:

in	*in, on*	States the idea of remaining in a place or time	Juan sta **in** camera sua (*Juan is in his bedroom*).
di	*of, from*	Gives the idea of possession, matter, or origin	La casa è **di** Gabriella (*The house belongs to Gabriela*). La sedia **di** legno (*The chair is made of wood*).
con	*with*	Indicates company	Sto **con** i miei amici (*I'm with my friends*).

1.2.   Practice

A. Complete the following sentences with the prepositions **in, di**, or **con**:

1.   Luigi vive _____ una grande città.

2. Maria viaggia sempre _____ sua sorella.

3. La casa è _____ colore giallo.

4. Le scarpe sono _____ pelle (*leather*).

5. Voi state _____ il capo.

6. Ci sono bei parchi _____ questa strada.

7. Il gatto è di _____ Pietro.

8. Mia nipote lavora _____ suo padre.

9. sto _____ Inghilterra.

B. Again, try to complete these sentences with **in, di,** or **con**

1. Flavia compie gli anni il quattro _____ aprile _____ 2000.

2. Vorrei un caffè _____ latte.

3. Questa cartella è _____ Simone.

4. Ritorna dall'ufficio _____ bicicletta.

5. Ho un bel rapporto _____ i miei genitori (*my parents*).

6. Ho una casa _____ otto finestre.

C. Try completing the sentences by choosing between **in** and **tra**

1. I miei nonni viaggiano (*drive*) _____ in auto per la città.

2. Tommaso sta _____ casa sua.

3. Filippo sta seduto (*sitting*) _____ Maria e Paolo.

4. Il signor Pérez ritorna a casa sua _____ le otto e le nove di sera.

5. Regaliamo un cane a Sebastiano _____ gli amici (*among the friends*).

6. I fiori sbocciano (*bloom*) _____ primavera.

2 OTHER COMMON PREPOSITIONS: A - PER - SENZA

a	*to*	Indicates movement towards a goal, whether real or imagined. It is used before an indirect object and a direct object when it's a person.	Vado **a** casa a piedi (I walk to my house). Parlo **a** mia sorella.
per	*for, in order to*	Indicates the aim or purpose of an action	La matita è **per** mia figlia (The pencil is for my daughter).
senza	*without*	Indicates lack of	L'hotel è **senza** turisti (The hotel is without tourists).

What follows a preposition?

⊃ In Italian, prepositions can be followed by verbs in the infinitive form: **Tommaso studia per imparare** (*Tomas studies to learn*) or **Martino parla senza pensare** (*Martin speaks without thinking*).

⊃ Prepositions can be followed by nouns: **Maria compra un fiore per sua madre** (*María buys a flower for her mother*).

⊃ Prepositions can be followed by pronouns: **Il libro è per lei** (*The book is for her*). In Italian, the pronouns that follow prepositions are **subject pronouns**, except for **me** and **te** (instead of **io** and **tu**): **Il caffè è per me** and **Il tè è per te**.

> When you use the preposition **con** together with the **1st and 2nd subject pronoun**, the result is **con me** and **con te**. In fact, **con** is the only preposition that combines with a pronoun. Example: **Mio marito viaggia sempre con me** (*My husband always travels with me*) or **Parlo con te nel parco** (*I talk with you in the park*).

2.1. Practice

A. Complete the following sentences with the prepositions **a, per**, or **senza**.

1. Il regalo è _____ Juan.

2. Mi piace il caffè _____ zuccherato

3. Il padre ritorna _____ a casa alle 9:00 di sera.

4. Lei studia _____ imparare.

5. Mia mamma _____ la sala.

6. Elena impara il tedesco _____ professori.

7. Mio zio entra _____ l'ufficio alle 8:00 del mattino.

8. Tommaso viaggia _____ mappe.

B. Complete the following sentences adding **a** just when it's needed:

1. José domanda _____ Maria quando torna sua mamma.

2. Per favore, descrivi _____ un leone.

3. Teresa cerca _____ i cani per dargli da mangiare.

4. Silvia dà calci _____ la porta.

5. Nell'oceano ci sono _____ pesci.

6. Parla _____ sua mamma.

C. Complete the following sentences choosing **a** or **di**.

1. Gli studenti ritornano _____ casa loro _____ le otto di sera.

2. Il martedì vado _____ Madrid.

3. Pietro fa esercizio _____ notte, non _____ giorno.

4. Sono le cinque _____ pomeriggio.

5. Sofía è _____ Cile.

6. Suo padre regala _____ sua figlia un cane.

7. Luigi viene _____ parlare con il dottore.

8. Quella bottiglia è _____ plastica.

D. Complete these sentences choosing between **da** and **di**.

1. Torna _____ la festa alle quattro del mattino.

2. Torna _____ casa a piedi dopo il lavoro.

3. Mi piacciono i piatti _____ legno.

4. Guardiamo la gente _____ dal balcone.

5. Studia in quel collegio _____ tre anni.

6. Vende vestiti _____ casa sua.

3 OTHER COMMON PREPOSITIONS: FINO A – DA/PER - SECONDO - PER - CONTRO

fino a	until, up to, as far as	Expresses a limit	Cammina **fino alla** cucina (*He/she walks up to the kitchen*).
da/per	by, for	Describes the means or cause for something. Also precedes a quantity of time.	Viaggia **in** barca (*He/she travels by boat*). Cammina **da** due ore (*She walks for two hours*).
secondo	according to	Used to describe the opinion of others. It's used before names and pronouns.	**Secondo** mia mamma, il film è brutto (*According to my mom, the film is bad*).
per	for, in order to	Used for deadlines, and to indicate purpose and destination	Il regalo è **per** la mia amica (*The present is for my friend*)
contro	against	Describes opposition	La lotta **contro** il cambiamento climatico (*The battle against climate change*)

3.1. Practice

A. See if you can complete these sentences with the right preposition from this last group: fino a - per – da - secondo - contro

1.   L'uomo salta _____ finestra.

2.   Il regalo è _____ suo figlio.

3.   _____ la mia amica, il ristorante non è buono.

4.   Camminiamo _____ parco.

5.   Lei guarda la TV _____ un'ora.

6.   Sono _____ le idee di quel professore.

7.   Sta a casa mia _____ martedì.

8.   C'è una camera da letto _____ due persone.

9.   _____ il dottore, devi mangiare molta verdura e frutta.

B. Complete the sentences with the right preposition from this list: **fino a - per - secondo - contro.**

1.   Questo oceano (*ocean*) arriva _____ coste africane (*the African coasts*).

2.   _____ mio fratello, oggi le banche sono chiuse.

3.   Per la Festa della Mamma, compro un regalo _____ mia mamma.

4.   Durante la gara (*race*), nuotano _____ la corrente (*against the current*)

5.   Nostro padre torna a casa _____ nove di sera.

6.   La barca naviga (*sails*) _____ Londra.

C. And now that you're more familiar with these prepositions, try to tackle the whole list with these sentences, filling in the blanks. These are the prepositions that you need:

a - tra - sopra - senza - con - per - secondo – fino a - da – su/sul - durante

1.   Non corro _____ scarpe da ginnastica.

2.   Maria porta la sua borsa _____ lei.

3.   Questi regali sono _____ i miei amici.

4.   _____ Paolo, il film non è bello.

5.   I bambini corrono _____ di noi.

6.   Il professore parla _____ fisica quantistica.

7.   Luigi corre _____ due ore

8.   Il libro sta _____ tavolo.

9.   L'auto sta _____ i due alberi.

10.   Parlo _____ mio padre.

ANSWER KEY ?

Practice. 1.1

A.   1. in 2. con 3. di 4. di 5. con 6. in 7. di 8. con 9. in

B.   1. di... di 2. con 3. di 4. in 5. con 6. con

C.   1. in 2. in 3. tra 4. tra 5. tra 6. in

Practice. 2.1

A.   1. per 2. senza 3. a 4. per 5. a 6. senza 7. a 8. senza

B.   1. a 2. X 3. a 4. X 5. X 6. a

C.   1. a... a 2. a 3. di... di 4. di 5. di 6. a 7. di 8. di

D.   1. di 2. da 3. di 4. da 5. da 6. da

Practice. 3.1

A.   1. da 2. per 3. secondo 4. fino a 5. da 6. contro 7. fino a 8. per 9. secondo

B.   1. fino a 2. secondo 3. per 4. contro 5. fino a 6. fino a

C.   senza 2. con 3. per 4. secondo 5. fino a 6. sopra 7. durante 8. su 9. tra 10. a

LESSON 15

PREPOSITIONS II

THE BOX IS BEHIND THE CHAIR

Did you think we were done with prepositions? There are so many of them, and they're all so important. Let's look at some more of them. These, in particular, are crucial for describing where something is located.

1 PREPOSITIONS FOR TALKING ABOUT PLACE AND POSITION

Compound prepositions are prepositions that are used to describe a **location** or **position**.

accanto a	*next to*
intorno a	*around*
vicino	*near*
sotto a	*underneath*

sotto	*under (more figurative than debajo de)*
davanti a	*before, in front of (physical location)*
di fronte	*before, in front of, in the presence of*
dentro a	*inside of*
dietro a	*behind*
dopo	*after (in a set of expressions)*
in cima a	*on top of*
faccia a faccia, di fronte	*in front of, opposite, facing, across from*
fuori da	*outside of*
vicino a, attaccato a	*close to, right next to*
lontano da	*far from*

Vocabulary: objects in a home

A great way to practice these new prepositions you've learned is by using them with common household objects. How is your home arranged? Can you describe it using the prepositions you just learned?

libreria	[lee-breh-ree-ah]	*bookcase*
scrittoio	[skreet-toh-yoh]	*desk*
sedia	[seh-dyah]	*chair*

computer	[kohm-pyoo-tehr]	*computer*
zaino	[tsah-eeh-noh]	*backpack*
quadro	[kwah-droh]	*picture*
orologio	[oh-roh-loh-joh]	*clock*
scaffale	[skahf-fah-leh]	*shelf*
giocattoli	[joh-kaht-toh-lee]	*toys*
palla	[pahl-lah]	*ball*
orso di peluche	[ohr-soh deeh peh-loo-cheh]	*stuffed teddy bear*
automobile	[ahw-toh-moh-bee-leh]	*car*
elicottero	[eh-lee-koht-teh-roh]	*helicopter*
matita/matite	[mah-tee-tah/mah-tee-teh]	*pencil/pencils*
portamatite	[pohr-tah-mah-tee-teh]	*pencil holder*
pianta	[pyahn-tah]	*plant*
scatola	[skah-toh-lah]	*box*
tappeto	[tahp-peh-toh]	*rug*

In Italian **di + il** contract to form **del: La via dell'ufficio postale** (*the street of the post office/ the post office street*) and **a + il** contract to form **al/alla: Cammina fino alla sala da pranzo** (*she walks up to the dining room*).

Notice that when **accanto a** precedes **il,** it becomes **accanto al.** The same happens with other prepositions.

1.1.   Practice

A. Fill in the blanks with the correct compound preposition:

1.   La palla sta _____ (inside of) la scatola.

2.   La palla sta _____ (outside of) scatola.

3.   La palla sta _____ (on top of) scatola.

4.   La palla sta _____ (underneath) la scatola.

5.   La palla sta _____ (right next to) scatola.

6.   La palla sta _____ (far from) scatola.

B. Give the opposites of these compound prepositions:

1.   Dentro al → _____

2.   Dietro al → _____

3.   Vicino al → _____

4.   In cima al → _____

5.   Accanto al → _____

C. Fill in the blanks with the correct compound preposition. Remember, that if the compound preposition has a **a** and is followed by the article **il**, you should contract both. Example: **La bambina sta <u>sotto all'albero</u> (sotto + a + il) árbol**

1.   L'auto sta _____ (behind) camion.

2.   Il portafoglio sta _____ (inside of) la borsa.

3.   La sedia sta _____ (in front of) tavolo.

4.   Lo zaino sta _____ (on top of) letto.

5.   Il gatto sta _____ (outside of) casa.

6.   Il cane dorme _____ (under) il ponte (*bridge*).

D. In this neighbourhood, there is a main square surrounded by a church, the post office and the town hall, one next to the other. Behind the post office is the movie theatre. There is a clock on top of the town hall. In the middle of the square there is a large park. On one of the sides of the square, there is a bar. The supermarket is twenty blocks away.

Choose a word from the first, second, and third column to form sentences. You're also going to need a verb. "Stare" is probably the verb to use. Though you may also use "C'è". Example: **La chiesa sta davanti alla piazza.**

la chiesa	lontano da	il bar
l'ufficio postale	vicino a	la chiesa
il municipio	dietro a	il cinema
il bar	sotto a	l'ufficio postale
il cinema	accanto a	il municipio
la piazza	davanti a	la piazza
il supermercato	sopra a	orologio

1. _____

2. _____

3. _____

4. _____

5. _____

E. Translate the following sentences describing where the objects in a room are located by using the right preposition. Example: The ball is next to the desk. **La palla sta _____ lo scrittoio.** **La palla sta accanto allo scrittoio.**

1. The chair is in front of the desk: La sedia sta _____ scrittoio.

2. The computer is on top of the desk: Il computer sta _____ lo scrittoio.

3. The plant is underneath the picture: La pianta sta _____ il quadro.

4. The toys are inside the box: I giocattoli stanno _____ scatola.

5. The stuffed teddy bear is in front of the box: L'orso di peluche sta _____ la scatola.

6. The red car is right next to the stuffed teddy bear: L'automobilina rossa sta _____ orso di peluche.

F. Translate the following sentences describing where the objects in a room are located by using the right preposition.

1. The backpack is far from the bookcase: Lo zaino sta _____ libreria.

2. The painting is near the bookcase: Il Quadro sta _____ biblioteca.

3. The pencils are inside the pencil holder: Le matite stanno _____ il portamatite.

4. The stuffed teddy bear is outside the box: L'orso di peluche sta _____ la scatola.

5. The map is on the wall: La mappa sta _____ parete.

6. The ball is under the desk: La palla sta _____ la scrivania.

2   EXPRESSING ORIGIN

In Italian you use the preposition **di** to express where you're from: **Sono del Perú** or **Voi siete del Belgio**.

And to ask where you're from, you need to use the preposition **di** + adverb **dove**, as in **Di dove sei tu?** (*Where are you from?*).

2.1.   Practice

A. Answer these questions according to the clues. Remember that you don't need to use the subject pronoun, as it is already implied in the verb form.

Example: **Di dove sei tu? (Francia). <u>Sono della Francia.</u>**

1.   Di dov'è il signor Pérez? (Inghilterra) _____

2.   Di dove sono io? (Stati Uniti) io → tu _____

3.   Di dove siete voi? (Italia) voi → noi _____

4.   Di dove sono Elena e Julio? (Canada) _____

5.   Di dove siamo noi? (Spagna) noi → voi _____

6.   Di dov'è Martino? (Germania) _____

7.   Di dove sono loro? (Belgio) _____

8.   Di dove sei tu? (Brasile) _____

3 GIVING AND FOLLOWING DIRECTIONS

Who doesn't need to know how to follow directions when traveling? It's useful to know how to in Italian. Some verbs you'll need to know are:

prendere	[prehn-deh-reh]	*to take*
seguire	[seh-gwee-reh]	*to continue*
guidare verso	[gwee-dah-reh vehr-soh]	*to drive forward*
svoltare	[svohl-tah-reh]	*to turn*
girare	[jee-rah-reh]	*to make a turn*
spiegare	[spee-eh-gah-reh]	*to explain*
arrivare	[ahr-ree-vah-reh]	*to reach*

---- Adverbs of Time ----

dopo (*after*)

poi (*after, then*)

allora (*then*)

mentre (*meanwhile/meantime*)

Vocabulary: the street

l'isolato	[lee-soh-lah-toh]	the block
la strada	[lah strah-dah]	the street
il viale	[eel vee-ah-leh]	the avenue
il marciapiede	[eel mahr-chee-ah-pee-eh-deh]	the sidewalk
la piazza principale	[lah pyaht-tsah preen-chee-pah-leh]	the main square
il semaforo	[eel seh-mah-foh-roh]	the traffic light
dritto	[dreet-toh]	straight
linea ferroviaria	[leeh-neh-ah fehr-roh-vee-ah-ryah]	the train tracks
a destra	[ah deh-strah]	to the right
a sinistra	[ah see-nee-strah]	to the left
l'angolo	[lahn-goh-loh]	the corner
la fermata del bus	[lah fehr-mah-tah dehl boohs]	the bus stop
nord	[nohrd]	north
sud	[sood]	south
ovest	[oh-vehst]	west

est	[ehst]	east
incrocio	[een-kroh-tschyoh]	the intersection
la rotonda	[lah roh-tohn-dah]	the traffic circle
la polizia	[lah poh-lee-tsee-ah]	the police
l'agente	[lah-jehn-teh]	the officer

3.1.   Practice

A. You're in a Italian-speaking city. How would you ask for these directions? **Example: Excuse me, could you please tell me where there is a public bathroom? <u>Mi scusi, può dirmi per favore dove sta un bagno pubblico?</u>**

1.   Please, can you tell me where the closest restaurant is?
     Per favore, sa dirmi _____?

2.   Excuse me, can you tell me how many blocks there are to the supermarket?
     Mi scusi, sa dirmi _____?

3.   Could you please tell me how to get to the main square?
     Mi scusi, sa dirmi _____?

4.   Excuse me, can you please tell me where the drugstore is?
     Mi scusi, sa dirmi per favore _____?

5.   Could you please tell me where the bus stop is?
     Mi scusi, sa dirmi _____?

B. Now see if you can translate the dialogue below.

—————— **Per strada** ——————

TERESA: Buongiorno, sa dove sta la banca?

AGENTE: Sì, le spiego. È a nord. Deve seguire questo viale fino a raggiungere l'incrocio. Poi deve svoltare a destra e procedere fino al semaforo, verso est.

TERESA: Quanti isolati sono fino al semaforo?

AGENTE: Sono cinque isolati fino al semaforo. Al semaforo, deve girare a sinistra, verso nord, e continuare per due isolati. Raggiunte una rotonda. La circonda e continua sulla stessa strada per un isolato. Poi deve girare a destra e procedere per altri sette isolati. Dopo svolta di nuovo a sinistra e procede per un altro isolato. La banca sta all'angolo, sulla destra.

TERESA: Grazie mille, agente. Spero di arrivarci!

C. You're in Italy and you want to help a lost tourist by giving them directions. Translate the following suggestions to Italian. **Example: You should turn left at the light → <u>Deve svoltare a sinistra al semaforo.</u>**

1.   You should continue on the avenue until you get to the corner:

_____

2.   You should take a right and continue straight:

_____

3.   You should continue straight until you reach the light:

_____

4.   You should make a turn at the light:

_____

5.   You should turn left and continue five blocks until you get to the main square:

_____

6.   You should drive forward until you get to the intersection:

_____

ANSWER KEY

Practice. 1.1

A.   1. dentro il 2. fuori de 3. sopra al 4. sotto 5. accanto a 6. lontano da

B.   1. fuori da 2. davanti a 3. lontano da 4. sotto a 5. lontano da

C.   1. L'auto sta dietro al camion. 2. Il portafoglio sta dentro la borsa. 3. La sedia sta davanti al tavolo. 4. Lo zaino sta sul letto. 5. Il gatto sta fuori dalla casa. 6. Il cane dorme sotto al ponte.

D.   1. L'ufficio postale sta accanto al municipio. 2. Il cinema sta dietro all'ufficio postale. 3. Il supermercato sta lontano dalla piazza. 4. Il bar sta davanti alla piazza. 5. Sopra al municipio c'è un orologio. 6. La chiesa sta vicino all'ufficio postale.

E.   1. La sedia sta di fronte allo scrittoio 2. Il computer sta sopra allo scrittoio 3. La pianta sta sotto al quadro 4. I giocattoli stanno dentro la scatola 5. L'orso di peluche sta davanti alla scatola. 6. L'automobilina rossa sta accanto all'orso di peluche

F.   1. Lo zaino sta lontano dalla libreria. 2. Il quadro sta vicino alla biblioteca. 3. Le matite stanno dentro al portamatite. 4. L'orso di peluche sta fuori dalla scatola. 5. La mappa sta sulla parete. 6. La palla sta sotto allo scrittoio.

Practice. 2.1

A.   1. È dell'Inghilterra. 2. Sei degli Stati Uniti. 3. Siamo dell'Italia. 4. Sono del Canada. 5. Siete della Spagna. 6. È della Germania 7. Sono del Belgio. 8. Io sono del Brasile.

Practice. 3.1

A.   1. Per favore, sa dirmi dove sta il ristorante più vicino? 2. Mi scusi, sa dirmi quanti isolati ci sono fino al supermercato? 3. Per favore, sa dirmi come arrivare alla piazza principale? 4. Mi scusi, sa dirmi per favore dove sta la farmacia? 5. Per favore, sa dirmi dove sta la fermata del bus?

B.   TERESA: Good morning. Do you know where the bank is?

C.   AGENTE: Yes, let me explain. It's towards the north. You need to follow this avenue until you reach the intersection. Then, turn right and keep on going until you reach the light, towards the east.

D.   TERESA: How many blocks are there until the streetlight?

E.   AGENTE: It's five blocks until the streetlight. At the light, you should turn left, towards north, and continue two blocks. You'll reach a traffic circle. Drive around it and continue on the same road for a block. Then turn right and keep going straight for seven blocks. Then turn left again and go one more block. The bank will be on the corner to the right.

F.   TERESA: Thank you very much, officer. I hope I get there!

G.   1. Deve seguire il viale fino all'angolo. 2. Deve prendere a destra e proseguire dritto. 3. Deve proseguire dritto fino al semaforo. 4. Deve girare al semaforo. 5. Deve svoltare a sinistra e proseguire per cinque isolati fino a raggiungere la piazza principale. 6. Deve procedere fino all'incrocio.

Printed in Great Britain
by Amazon

29895084R00123